UNCLE SAM
Pages 60, 61

CANUCKY
Pages 57, 58, 59

FLORAL RHAPSODY
Pages 18, 19

Copyright © 1993 Susan Scheewe Publications, Inc.
13435 NE Whitaker Way, Portland, Oregon 97230
Phone (503) 254-9100

SERENDIPITY:
Discovering things desirable or of value unexpectedly or by accident.

This book was a lot of fun and very rewarding, creating projects that are somewhat unusual or unexpected.

I think we all like to have unique items in our homes. Collectibles that will become family treasures. It was keeping this in mind that I began to "play".

I hope you will be pleased with the results and as always be inspired to create your own....

"Serendipity Collectibles".

Much love and laughter....

Thank you Kevin Truscott for getting me to sit still long enough to snap this photo!

If you enjoy decorative painting and sharing ideas with others, you should consider joining the National Society of Tole and Decorative Painter.

For information write to:
NSTDP
P. O. Box 808
Newton, Ks. 67114

Rights to this book have been reserved. No part of book to be reproduced in printed form without written consent of publisher. Designs may be painted on projects for fun and for profit.

IMPORTANT: Please be sure to thoroughly read the instructions for all products used to complete projects in this book, paying particular attention to all cautions and warnings shown for that product to ensure their proper and safe use.

SUPPLIES

BASIC SUPPLIES

Sponge Brushes
Tracing Paper (for tracing patterns from book)
Graphite and White Transfer Paper (for transferring pattern)
Stylus
Tack Cloth
Sandpaper
Scotch Magic Tape
Lint Free Paper Towels
9" x 12" Waxed Disposable Palette Pad for Acrylics
Palette Knife
Water Basin
Rulers
Rags for antiquing if desired
Durhams Wood Putty
Wood Filler
Wood Glue

BRUSHES

Round: Stan Brown's Size 4
Liner: Stan Brown's Size 0
Shader: Royal 3/4", Robert Simmons 2, 12, Stan Brown's 8,10,
Mop Brush: Robert Simmons 1/2" and small
Fan Brush: Robert Simmons
Deerfoot Stippler: 1/4" Bette Byrd
Grainer Brush: Stan Brown's 1/4" and Royal 1/2"

WOOD AND POT BELLIES SOURCES

Stan Brown's Arts and Crafts
13435 N. E. Whitaker Way
Portland, Oregon 97230

Information and Gourd Sources:
American Gourd Society Inc.
Box 274K
Mount Gilead, Oh. 43338-0274

BASIC WOOD PREPARATION

1. Sand wood. Fill all holes with wood filler.
2. Remove dust with a tack cloth. Apply sealer of choice.
3. Sand lightly taking care to not remove sealer. Be careful to not make surface too smooth or paint will not adhere.

TIN

1. Wipe entire tin with white vinegar and water to clean.
   Carefully remove all dirt, rust, paint, etc.
   Be sure surface is dry.
2. Tin may then be basecoated with Penetrol if desired.
   Tin may also be sprayed with a paint such as Rustoleum Spray Enamel. Both work well to stop rust.

FINISHES

All of the pieces in this book have been sprayed with four to five light coats of Blair Harvest Tole Matte or Satin varnish. Let dry well between coats. Use tweezers to remove any unwanted particles that may settle in varnish. Use adequate ventilation.

PAINTS

As you can see I like a wide variety of colors and brands. I like different things about all of them. Feel free to improvise and make substitutions.

ANTIQUING

There are many different ways to antique. See each project for specific details.

I usually dip a soft rag into oil paint and spread as smoothly as possible over desired area to be antiqued. Use thinner to highlight desired areas.

GLOSSARY OF TERMS

BASECOATING: Applying a smooth layer of paint. It should be opaque. It will take two to three coats to achieve desired effect. To avoid ridges start from the middle of design and work to edge. It is better to have multiple thin coats than thick coats. Make sure paint is dry (does not feel cool to the touch) between layers. You may also sand lightly between coats with a very fine sandpaper if desired.

FLOATING OR SIDELOADING: This is what I use extensively for all shading. Practice to achieve a soft, blended look.

Dip your clean brush into water. Blot the excess water out on paper towels. Dip the side of your brush in paint and blend on the palette. Do not let the paint travel completely across the brush. If your brush is correctly loaded the paint will gradually blend from the paint side to a a clear water side. This will take a little practice. The brush must not be too wet or too dry. Be patient, it is well worth the effort.

DOUBLELOAD: Completely load your brush with base color. Dip edge into another color. Blend back and forth on palette.

WASH OR GLAZE: Thin paint down with water and brush over completed area. It should be quite transparent.

STIPPLING: I like to use a deerfoot stippler although your old worn out brushes work well too. Use a straight up and down pouncing motion on desired area. Brush must be dry.

TRANSFERRING PATTERNS: The main thing to remember is transfer only the lines that are necessary. Be careful to not press too hard as this may damage the surface. Basecoat must be cured before tracing, allow adequate time.

SPATTERING: I like to use a fan brush dipped into slightly thinned paint then tapped with another brush. I find this method somewhat easier to control. Be careful when spattering to not do too much and lose the effect you are striving for.

STYLUS: This is used for transferring the design through the graphite. I also use it to make stylus dots and hearts.

Color Comparison Chart

All symbols key on the DecoArt color:
A (+) by another company's color means that the color family is the same, but the other company's color is darker than DecoArt.
A (-) by another company's color means that the color family is the same, but the other company's color is lighter than DecoArt.
An (*) by the DecoArt color means that no other company has a reasonably comparative color to our knowledge.

These comparisons were compared dry to dry. As some companies vary their colors slightly in different batches, please be aware that the colors will be close but seldom exact. This color comparison chart is as close as represenative samples as possible, however, DecoArt does not guarantee the identical color matches of competitive colors. This is only a general guide for comparison.

COLORS	DECOART AMERICANA (DA)	DELTA CERAMCOAT	PLAID FOLKART	ILLINOIS BRONZE ACCENT & COUNTRY COLORS
WHITES	DA1 Snow White		901 Wicker White	2476 Real White
	DA2 White Wash	E White		2454 White Wash
	DA3 Buttermilk	2001 Antique White	903 Tapioca	2428 Off White
	DA4 Sand	2036 Ivory	902 Taffy	2311 Adobe Wash
	DA77 Desert Sand		703 Vanilla Cream	
	DA89 Cool Neutral	2402 Sandstone	857 Porcelain White	
	DA90 Warm Neutral		704 Milkshake	
YELLOWS	(*)DA5 Taffy Cream			
	DA6 Pineapple	2005 Pale Yellow		
	(*)DA7 Moon Yellow			2306 Cactus Flower
	DA8 Yellow Ochre	(-)2092 Old Parchment	737 Butter Crunch	
	DA9 Antique Gold	2003 Oaktone		
	DA10 Cadmium Yellow	D Yellow		
	DA11 Lemon Yellow	2064 Sunbright Yellow	(+)918 Sunny Yellow	2410 Mellow Yellow
		(+)2027 Bright Yellow	735 Lemon Custard	
		2004 Luscious Lemon		
		(-)2101 Pineapple		736 School Bus Yellow
	(*)DA93 Raw Sienna			
ORANGES	DA12 Tangerine	2028 Native Flesh		
	DA13 Pumpkin	2042 Pumpkin		2473 True Orange
		(+)2026 Orange		
	DA14 Cadmium Orange	(+)2043 Tangerine		2573 Floral Orange
	(*)DA15 Cadmium Red		920 Autumn Leaves	
	DA16 Burnt Orange	2097 Georgia Clay		
	DA17 Georgia Clay	2030 Burnt Sienna		
		2020 Red Iron Oxide		
	DA102 Medium Flesh	2126 Medium Flesh		2420 Peaches 'n Cream

COLORS	DECOART AMERICANA (DA)	DELTA CERAMCOAT	PLAID FOLKART	ILLINOIS BRONZE ACCENT & COUNTRY COLORS
REDS	DA18 Country Red	2098 Tomato Spice	931 Red Clay	2302 Pueblo Red
	DA19 Berry Red	2107 Tompt Red	932 Calico Red	2470 Pure Red
				2449 Jo Sonja Red
	DA20 Calico Red	C Bright Red		2579 Razzle Red
	DA21 Crimson Tide	2075 Maroon	758 Cherry Royale	2332 Bordeaux
	DA22 Burgundy Wine		935 Raspberry Wine	2421 Holiday Red
		2130 Sweetheart Blush	(-)957 Burgundy	
		2125 Pthalo Crimson		
	DA79 Brandy Wine	2123 Burgundy Rose	847 Apple Spice	
	DA80 Russet	2407 Candy Bar	757 Brownie	
	DA96 Red Iron Oxide	2020 Red Iron Oxide	914 Rusty Nail	2424 Barn Red
	DA97 Rookwood Red	2446 Sonoma	756 Chocolate Cherry	2425 Fingerberry Red
	(*)DA104 Naphtol Red	2408 Napthol Crimson		
	DA112 Cranberry Wine		935 Raspberry Wine	
PINKS MAUVES PURPLES	DA23 Peaches & Cream	(-)2433 Island Coral	(+)911 Apricot Cream	2319 L 'Orangerie
	DA24 Flesh	(-)2033 Dresden Flesh	752 Berries 'N Cream	2452 Victorian Mauve
	DA25 Dusty Rose	(-)2018 Indiana Rose	(-)929 Cotton Candy	2450 Roseberry
		2432 Normandy Rose	753 Rose Chiffon	
	DA26 Mauve	2132 Bouquet	(-)912 Promenade	
	DA27 Gooseberry	2129 Gypsy Rose		
	DA28 Raspberry	2405 Dusty Mauve		
	(*)DA29 Boysenberry			
	DA30 Spice Pink		955 Sweetheart Pink	
	(*)DA31 Baby Pink			
	(*)DA32 Lilac	(+)2403 Lilac Dust		
	DA33 Orchid	2060 Lilac		
	DA34 Lavender		(-)933 Heather	2475 True Purple
	DA101 Dioxazine Purple	2015 Purple		2204 Purple Canyon
	DA103 Coral Rose	2045 Fiesta Pink		
	DA110 Blush			

COLORS	DECOART AMERICANA (DA)	DELTA CERAMCOAT	PLAID FOLKART	ILLINOIS BRONZE ACCENT & COUNTRY COLORS		COLORS	DECOART AMERICANA (DA)	DELTA CERAMCOAT	PLAID FOLKART	ILLINOIS BRONZE ACCENT & COUNTRY COLORS
BLUES	DA35 Navy Blue	2114 Midnight	908 Indigo	2446 Indigo Blue		BROWNS	DA58 Antique White	(-)2402 Sandstone	(+)939 Butter Pecan	2453 Wicker
	DA36 True Blue	(-)2124 Manganese Blue		2472 Pure Blue			DA59 Toffee	2085 AC Flesh		
		2089 Navy Blue		2412 Ultra Marine Blue			DA60 Mocha	(-)2019 Fleshtone		
		2051 Copen Blue					DA61 Sable Brown	2425 Territorial Beige		
		B Phalo Blue					DA62 Terra Cotta	(+)2055 Autumn Brown		
	DA37 Blueberry	2131 Nightfall						2086 Toffee		
	(*)DA38 Wedgewood Blue						DA63 Burnt Sienna	2023 Brown Iron Oxide	945 Maple Syrup	2435 Burnt Sienna
	DA39 Victorian Blue								943 Molasses	
	DA40 Williamsburg Blue	(-)2069 Wedgewood Blue		2440 Stoneware Blue			DA64 Burnt Umber	2053 Dark Brown	940 Coffee Bean	2408 Sweet Chocolate
		2133 Cape Cod					DA65 Dark Chocolate	2024 Walnut	950 Chocolate Fudge	
	(*)DA41 Country Blue							2025 Burnt Umber		2437 Burnt Umber
	DA42 Baby Blue	2037 Blue Heaven					DA78 Flesh Tone	2125 Medium Flesh	949 Skintone	
	(*)DA43 Salem Blue						DA91 Cashmere Beige	2033 Dresden Flesh	705 Almond Parfait	
	DA44 Desert Turquoise	2058 Colonial Blue					DA02 Mink Tan	2424 Bambi	/06 Chocolait Parfait	
	DA81 Colonial Green			2451 Village Green			DA94 Mississippi Mud	2109 Brown Velvet		2436 Raw Sienna
	DA85 Midnight Blue	2413 Prusian Blue	964 Midnight	2439 Liberty Blue			DA109 Taupe			
	DA86 Uniform Blue	2114 Midnight	(+)975 Slate Blue	2441 Soldier Blue			DA114 Lt. Cinnamon			
	DA87 Indian Turquoise		729 Baby Blue	(+)2307 Nevada Turquoise		BLACKS	DA67 Ebony Black	F Black	938 Licorice	2477 Real Black
	DA98 French Blue	2133 Cape Cod		2440 Stoneware Blue		GREYS	(*)DA88 Charcoal Grey			
	(*)DA99 Sapphire						(*)DA68 Slate Grey	(+)2426 Cadet Grey		
	DA100 Ultra Deep Blue	2038 Ultra Marine Blue					DA69 Dove Grey	2090 Hippo Grey		
	DA105 Blue Grey Mist		718 Blue Gray Dust				(*)DA95 Neutral Grey			
	DA115 Blue Haze			2310 Prairie Green			DA111 Grey Sky			
GREENS	DA45 Mint Julep		(+)915 Robin's Egg			METALLICS	DA70 Shimmering Silver		No Comparable Product	
	(*)DA46 Sea Aqua						DA71 Glorious Gold		No Comparable Product	
	DA47 Bluegrass Green		725 Tartan Green	2577 Holiday Green			DA72 Venetian Gold		No Comparable Product	
	DA48 Holly Green	2115 Blue Spruce		2310 Prairie Green			DA73 Bronze		No Comparable Product	
	DA49 Dark Pine	2068 Christmas Green					DA74 Royal Ruby		No Comparable Product	
	(*)DA50 Forest Green	2100 Woodland Night					DA75 Ice Blue		No Comparable Product	
	DA51 Leaf Green	2420 Dark Jungle	927 Old Ivy	2442 Green Olive			DA76 Crystal Green			
			926 Shamrock							
	DA52 Avacado	2420 Dark Jungle	952 Ripe Avocado	2320 Chateau Moss		SPECIALIZED PRODUCTS	DAS1 Brush 'n Blend (Extender)	8001 Acry Blend	947 Extender	
			(*)928 Patchwork Green				DAS10 Fabric Painting Medium	300 Textile Medium	704 Fabric Medium	
			(-)923 Clover				DAS11 Control Medium (Thickner)		940 Thickner	
GREENS	DA53 Mistletoe	2011 Chrome Greebn Lt.								
	(*)DA54 Bright Green									
	DA55 Kelly Green	2008 Green Isle								
	DA56 Olive Green	2067 Leaf Green	954 Fresh Foliage	2445 Pine Needle Green						
	DA57 Jade Green	(+)2422 Leprechaun	922 Bayberry							
		2070 Wedgewood Green								
	DA62 Evergreen	2010 Forest Green	924 Thicket	2444 Deep Forest Green						
	DA63 Black Forest	2096 Dark Forest	727 Parrot Green							
	DA64 Midnight Green	2116 Black Green	925 Wrought Iron							
	DA106 Lt. Avocado		728 Green Olive	2438 Chesapeake Blue						
	(*)DA108 Viridian Green	A Pthalo Green								
	DA113 Plantation Pine		730 Southern Pine	2438 Chesapeake Blue						
	DA116 Deep Teal									

DecoArt™

Box 360, Stanford, KY 40484 (606)365-3193 Toll-Free (800)367-3047 Fax (606)365-9739

10 PREPARATION OF GOURDS

CLEANING:

To clean gourds simply wash in a large bucket or sink with a scrub brush, warm water and a little elbow grease. I find a plastic pan scraper works well on stubborn areas. The mold comes off surprisingly easy. Next wipe gourds with a bleach and water dampened cloth. Let continue curing if necessary.

TO FOOT A GOURD OR POTBELLY

Draw a chalk line up the center of gourd. This will help you position the feet. Make a thick, workable clay using Durham's wood putty compound and water. Only mix enough clay for one gourd at a time.

Form into a suitable base. Use your palette knife to crease between feet. Make sure feet are flush at the back of gourd and not sticking out too far.

Place gourd in position and let dry on wax paper. Gourds should pop off when dry.

At this point you may wish to mix up more clay and build up feet if too flat. Let dry well. Glue feet to gourd. If shrinkage occurs, fill cracks with wood filler. Wood filler also works well in areas there may be unwanted dents or cracks You may wish to spray clay areas with a light misting of Krylon Matte finish before basecoating.

Sand feet and your Santa is ready to come to life!

If your gourd's stem has broken off or does not have one, carefully drill a hole in end of gourd and glue in a new stem.

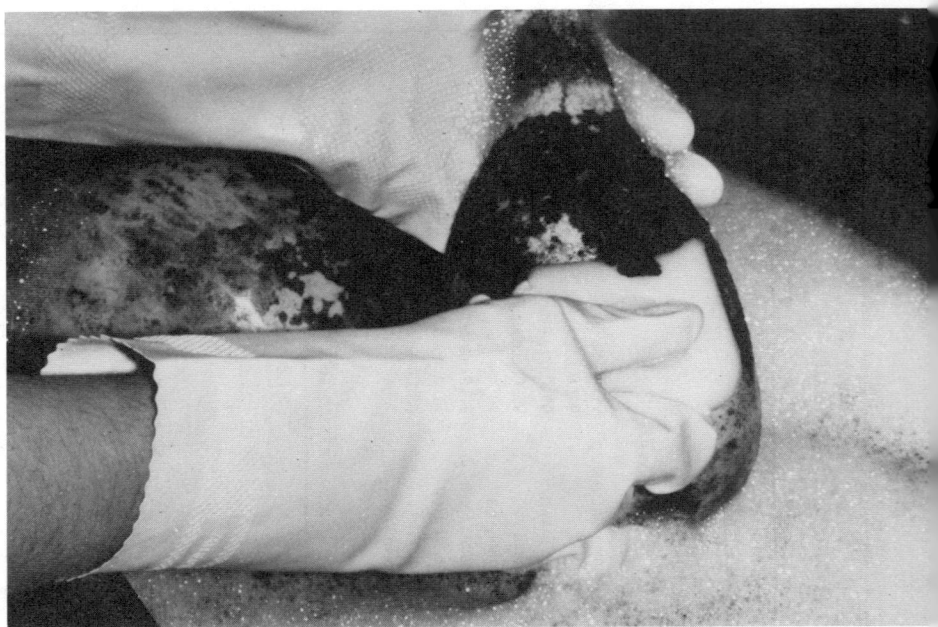

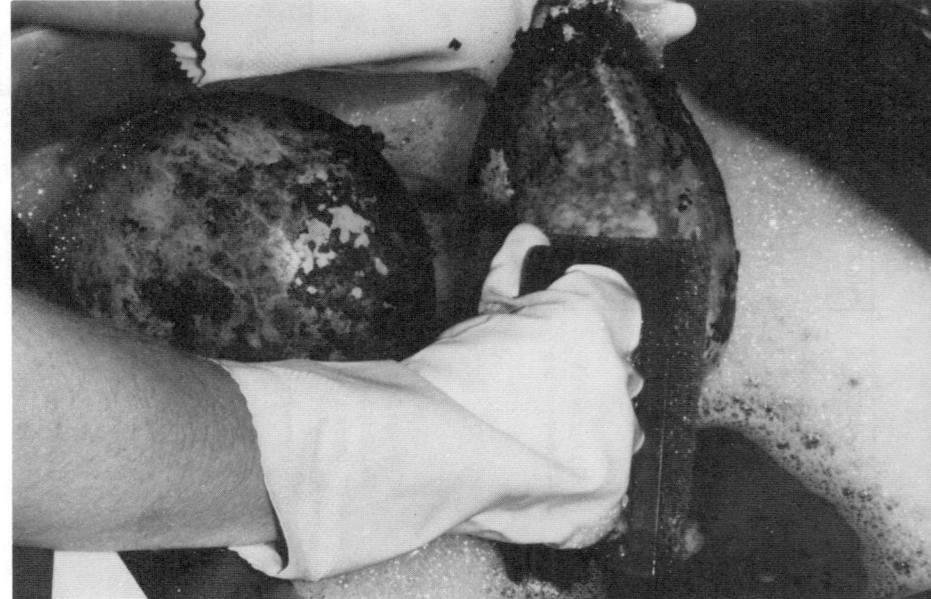

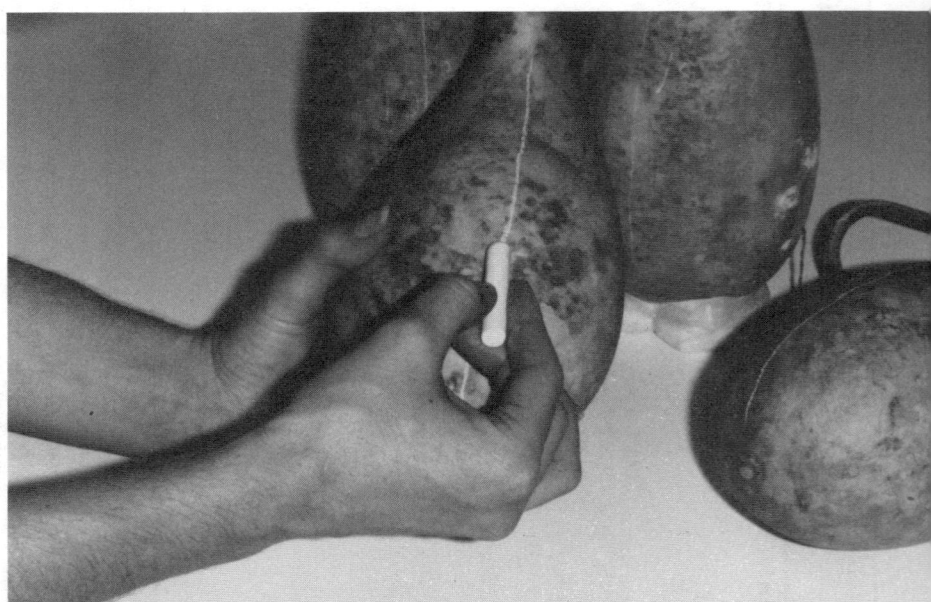

Simply "Gourdgeous"

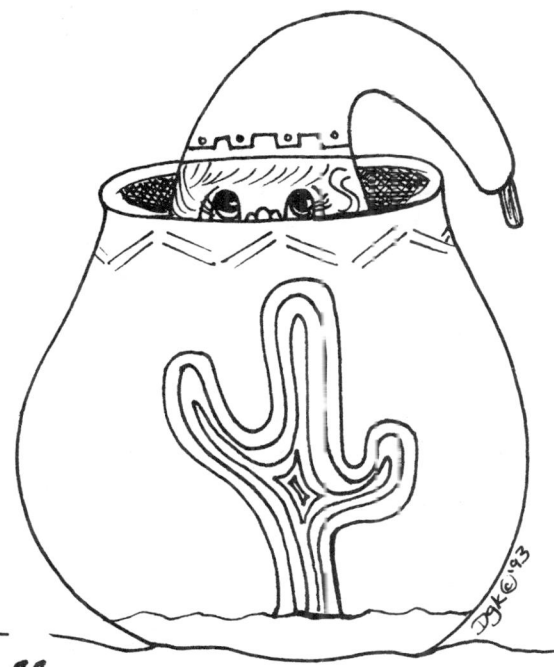

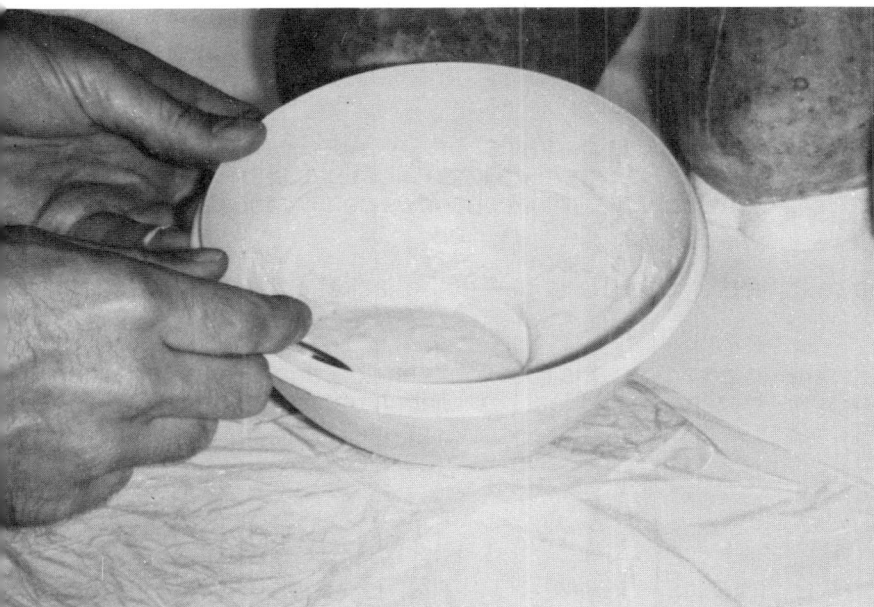

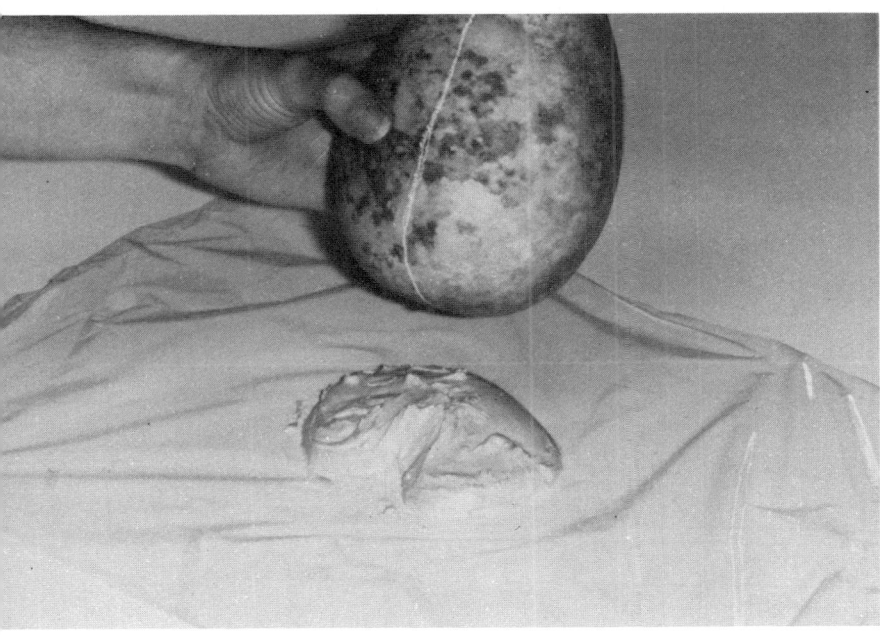

BASIC SANTA GOURD OR POTBELLY INSTRUCTIONS

THESE PATTERNS MAY ALSO BE PAINTED ON POTBELLIES IF DESIRED.

1. Be sure gourd is clean and dry. Base gourd and feet in desired colors. Transfer on basic pattern lines lightly avoiding details. Adjust pattern sizes accordingly. Place face high on gourd so it doesn't appear too wide. The shoulders should be a bit lower than the waist.
    Helpful Hint: For waists or coat hems, etc. place gourd on a flat, level surface. Rest your hand on edge and lightly mark with chalk while slowly turning gourd.

2. **FACE**
    Base face Medium Flesh. Lightly trace on facial markings. Float Burnt Sienna around face features such as eyelids, nose and wrinkles. Float Burnt Sienna so paint flows up above markings. Keep soft looking. See Worksheet No. 1.

3. Base eyes White. Base irises indicated color. Add pupils in Black. Float on left side of irises with desired shade to add depth. Use a fine liner to outline eyes and lashes with thinned Raw Umber.

4. Float desired color wash over cheek area and underside of nose. Float cheek color with paint side towards mouth. Moisten gourd first and blend well - no harsh lines! Highlight top of nose and eyelids with Fleshtone. Add Snow White dry brush highlights to eyes and cheeks. Use a liner and thinned Snow White to apply twinkle to eyes if desired.

5. Base open mouth area with Candy Bar. Using a small shader double load Medium Flesh and cheek color for lower lip.

6. Base hair and beard with Hippo Grey. Use a rake comb brush or grainer brush. Add layer of Quaker Grey then Snow White. Follow line drawing for hair growth pattern. Be careful to keep all values showing. Use liner brush for moustache and eyebrows and and also for fine hair details. Float shadows below moustache and hat with Hippo Grey. Keep soft looking. See Worksheet No. 2.

7. Fine liner strokes of White may have to be reapplied to beard and hair along jacket if this area becomes muddy looking.

8. When floating shadows around arms make sure to also float shadow lightly inside arm area everywhere except upper forearm. This will make the arm look more dimensional. Float highlight on upper forearms.

PUNCHED TIN AND HOLLYHOCKS

PALETTE
Delta Ceramcoat
Charcoal   Black Green
Maple Sugar   Dark Forest
Light Ivory
Folk Art Metallic
Sterling Silver
Deco Art Americana
Gooseberry Pink
Calico Red

1. Sand and seal birdhouse with MinWax Early American stain. Sand again lightly.
2. Copy pattern onto tracing paper. Tape to one side of roof. Use a nail and hammer to make holes. Reverse pattern and repeat on other side of roof.
3. Basecoat roof Charcoal. Use a liner brush to get Charcoal into every hole. When dry brush over with a coat of Sterling Silver. Use a dry flat brush and take off excess paint onto a paper towel. This will allow some of the Charcoal to show through giving a realistic tin appearance.
4. Use an old flat brush for the hollyhocks foliage. Load brush in Dark Forest and then corner load in Black Green. Use chisel edge of brush with Black Green side out. See example.
5. Put out dollops of Maple Sugar, Light Ivory, Gooseberry Pink and Calico. Load a Q-tip in one color and then dip a part into one or more other colors. Use a straight up and down motion. The indentation left is the flower center.
6. The vines are liner strokes of Dark Forest.
7. Let birdhouse dry well. Apply Glazing and Blending Medium with a soft rag to stain areas. Rub in well. Blend in Burnt Umber oil paint with a brush around the base of flowers, around hole and under roof line. Blend well. Let cure for a day or two and spray varnish.

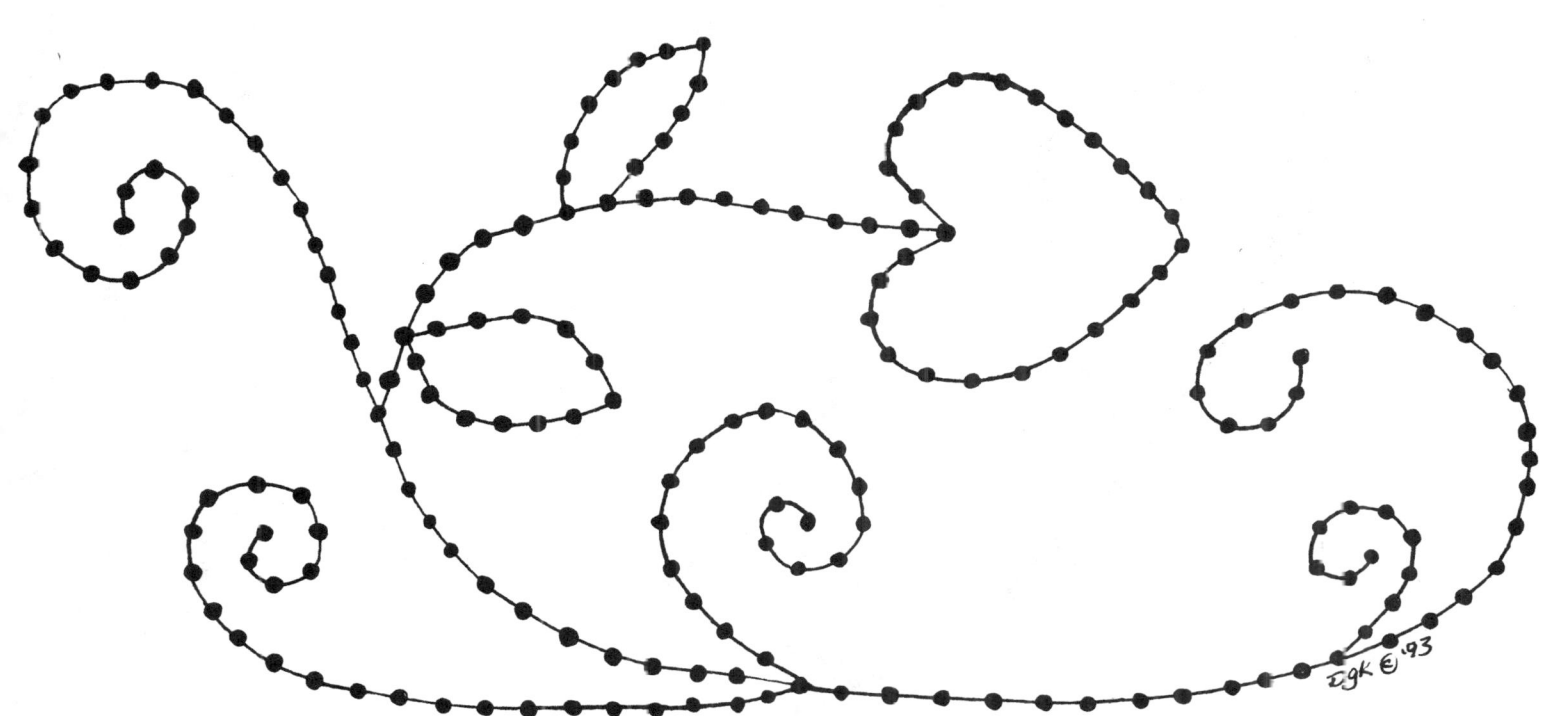

REVERSE FOR OTHER SIDE OF ROOF

LOVEBIRD STOOL

LOVEBIRD STOOL

PALETTE
Folk Art
Metallic Sterling Silver
Raspberry Wine
Delta Ceramcoat
Charcoal
Accent Country Colors
Soldier Blue

1. Stain bar stool Walnut. Sand lightly. Copy pattern onto tracing paper. Center and tape to stool top.
2. Use a hammer and nail (I used a 1-1/4" roofing nail) to punch in holes 1/8" deep following pattern. Leave space between holes.
3. Sand lightly and wipe with tack cloth.
4. Basecoat top and sides of stool top with Charcoal. Use your liner brush to get in all of the holes. This will probably take two coats. Let dry well.
5. Pour Sterling Silver onto a palette. Use a wide flat shader. Fill dry brush and then wipe on paper towel to remove excess paint. Do not have too much paint on brush. Brush back and forth over sides and top of stool. Some Charcoal will show through making your stool look just like authentic punched tin. Take your time working from the inside of the pattern out.
6. Paint decorative rounds of stool legs. I used Raspberry Wine on one and Soldier Blue on the other.

This pattern would look great as a clock, or try it on a large plate!

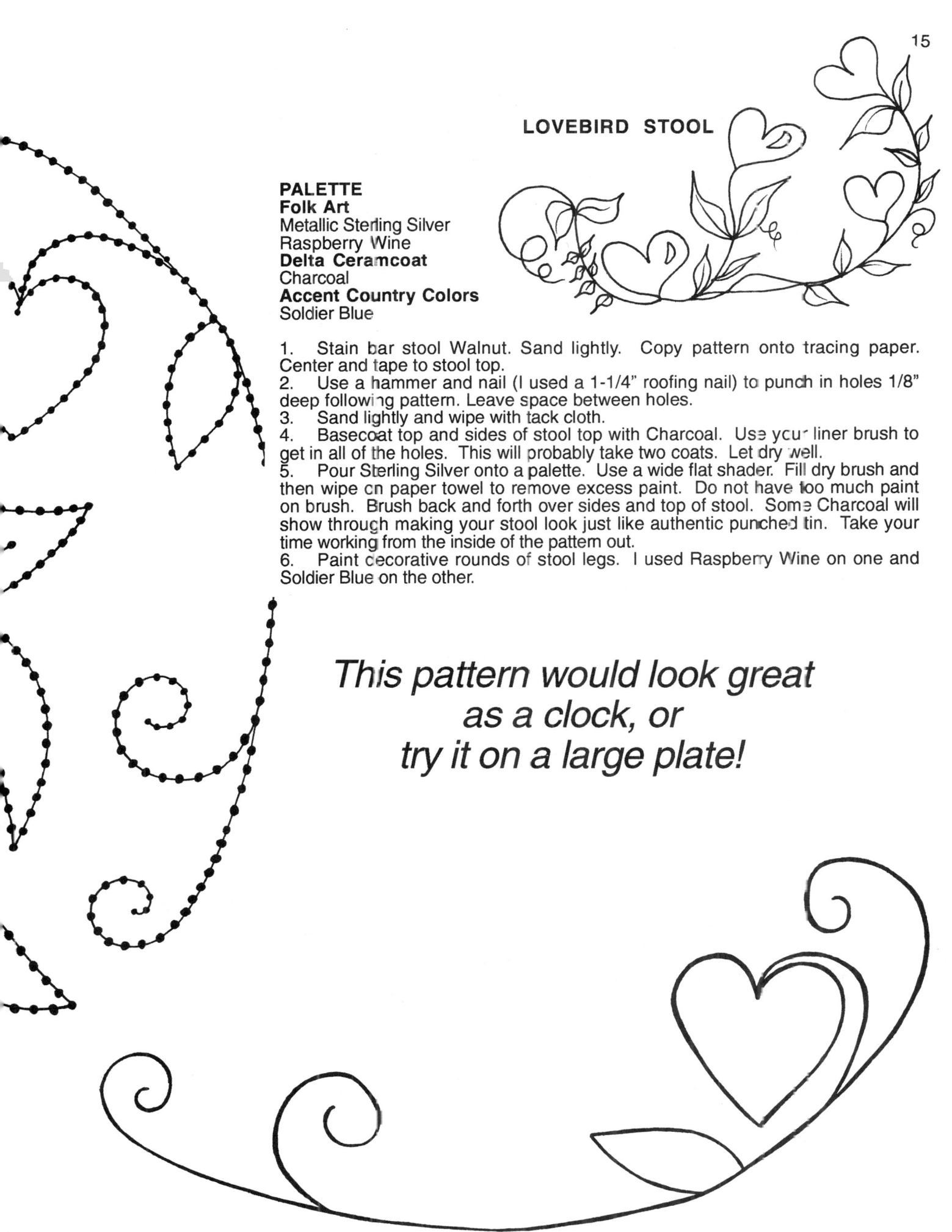

SLEDDIN' SANTA

PALETTE
Deco Art Americana
Medium Flesh   Snow White
Ebony Black   Ultra Blue Deep
Leaf Green   Calico Red
Deco Art Heavy Metals
Glimmer (clear)
Deco Art Dazzling Metallics
Venetian Gold
Deco Art Hot Shops
Fiery Red
Thermal Green
Delta Ceramcoat
Fleshtone   Charcoal
Black Green   Burnt Sienna
Hippo Grey   Quaker Grey
Accent County Colors
Raw Umber
Folk Art
Raspberry Wine
Baby blue
Fold Art Metallic
Sterling Silver
Jo Sonja
Rich Gold

1. Take Santa and sled apart. Sand and seal all pieces except for sled with Jo Sonja All Purpose Sealer. Sand again lightly. Sand and stain sled with MinWax Early American Stain. Sand again lightly.
2. Basecoat Santa's coat and hat with Antique Gold. Then apply two coats of Calico Red. Crinkle Saran Wrap and dip into a puddle of Raspberry Wine. Blot off excess. Apply all over hat and coat, taking care to leave plenty of Calico Red showing through. When dry, dip a fresh piece of Saran Wrap into Rich Gold and dab over coat and hat.
3. Follow basic Santa face instructions. Eyes are Baby Blue floated with Ultra Blue Deep. Cheeks are a Calico wash floated above the moustache. Float a Burnt Sienna wash over forehead and by hairline.
4. Basecoat pants with Raspberry Wine. Float below coat cur with Charcoal.
5. Basecoat boots with Charcoal. Float shading on top of boots with Ebony Black. Bottom of soles are Ebony Black as well. Add Snow White highlights to boots.
6. Float shading above fur line on coat and hat with Raspberry Wine. Also, flat around shoulder area.
7. Basecoat mitts with Leaf Green. Float shading below fur cuff with Black Green.
8. Use a rake brush to apply Charcoal to all fur areas. Keep both sides of fur edges uneven. Use a dry deerfoot stippler to pounce Sterling Silver over the Charcoal areas. Then go over that with Snow White. Be careful to keep all three values showing.
9. Basecoat the tree with Leaf Green. The edges and bottom are Black Green. Stipple at branch divisions with Snow White.
10. Basecoat berries on sled with Antique Gold and then Calico Red. Highlight with Fiery Red. Dry brush in Snow White shine areas. Outline berries with a thin Charcoal line. Basecoat holly with Leaf Green. Add scroll work using Black Green. Float shading on holly with Black Green. Highlight with Thermal Green. Use the end of your paint brush to make Black Green dots along curved edge of sled.
11. Brush Glimmer (clear) over berries, fur and tree.
12. Apply Blending and Glazing Medium to sled with a soft cloth. Rub in well. Apply Burnt Umber oil paint with an old brush for shading. Follow along where the Santa would lie on the sled. Also, shade base of curved area of sled and tree trunk. Blend in well. Let cure one to two days. Assemble Santa and spray varnish. Spatter Snow White on sled. Spray varnish with several coats.

FLORAL RHAPSODY

PALETTE
Delta Ceramcoat
Antique White   Hydrangea
Lavender   Alpine
Green Sea   Woodland Night
Straw Laguna
Deco Art Americana
Country Blue
Snow White
Folk Art
Teal Green   Potpourri Rose
Spring Rose   Lavender Sachet
Heather   Raspberry Wine
Dazzling Metallics Deco Art
Ice Blue
Glorious Gold
Deco Art Hot Shots
Fiery Red
Accent Country Colors
Deep Forest Green

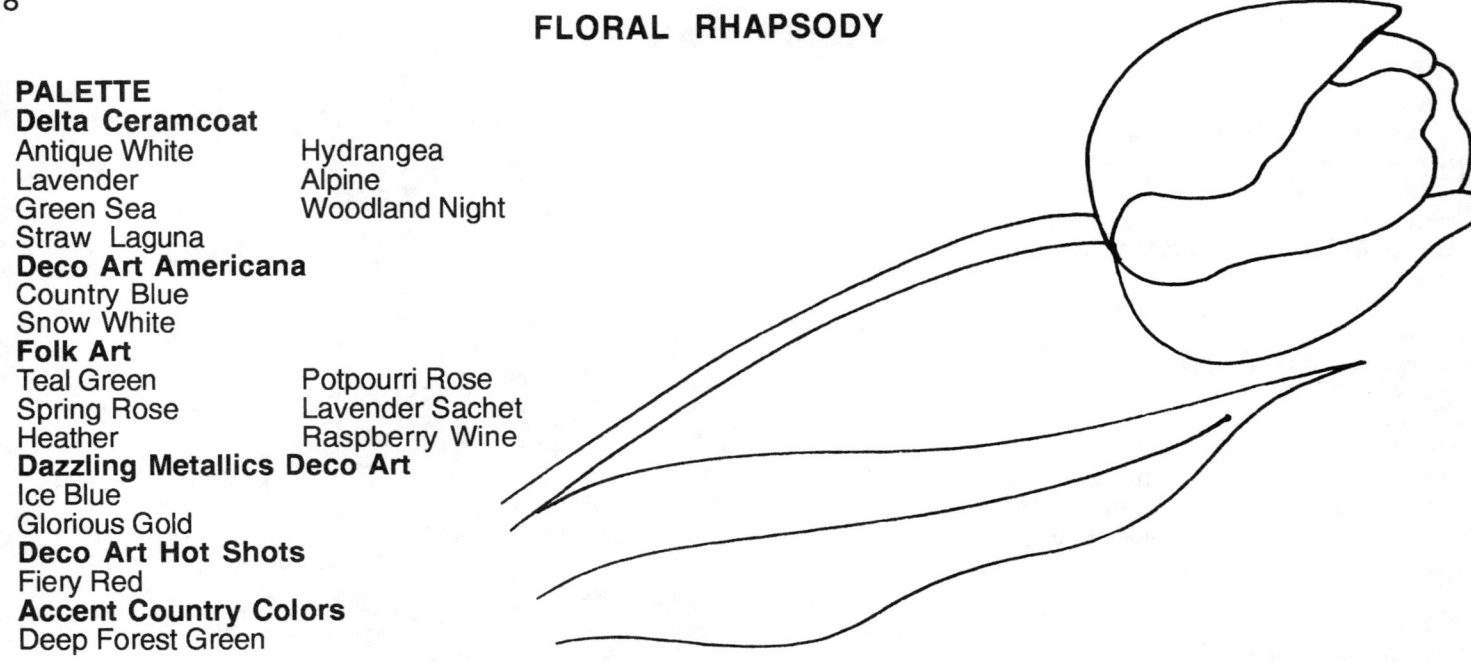

1. This gourd has a 31" circumference. Adapt to fit your gourd size by omitting or adding space between tulips.
2. Basecoat total gourd Antique White.
3. Resting your hand on a steady surface, twirl gourd slowly while marking a chalkline approximately halfway up the gourd. Basecoat bottom of gourd Ice Blue. Use a rake brush at the center to feather the line.
4. Lightly transfer pattern avoiding details.
5. Basecoat tulip stems and leaves Teal Green. Float shading and outline with Deep Forest Green. Highlight leaves with Laguna and Heather washes.
6. Basecoat alternately two tulips Hydrangea and two tulips Potpourri Rose. Shade and outline Hydrangea roses with Raspberry. Highlight with Fiery Red wash. Shade and outline the Potpourri Rose with Raspberry and highlight with Hydrangea.
7. Use a medium permanent Black pen for the musical compositions. It is easier to simply draw on the notes using my pattern as an example only, instead of drying to transfer the details. Write your own composition!
8. The forget-me-nots are so easy and fun to do. Use the wooden end of your liner brush. Dab in paint and make flower dots in and amongst tulips and musical compositions. Let dry well taking care not to smear. Put out dollops of Lavender, Potpourri Rose, Spring Rose, Lavender Sachet, Heather and Country Blue. Make the forget-me-nots interesting by using combinations of the above colors.
   When the flowers are dry use stylus dipped in Straw for the centers. The leaves are stroke marks of Alpine, Green Sea and Woodland Nights. Don't clean brush. Allow colors to intermingle. It will make the leaves move interesting.
9. Create a loose scallop like pattern of small Snow White stylus dots underneath the entire floral pattern. Stop occasionally to make sure you are pleased with the pattern.
10. Do a freehand wide float of Snow White in a soft curing scallop along top upper portion of gourd. Small White stylus dot line underneath the wide float.
11. When spraying with varnish use light coats or else the Black permanent pen may tend to run.

Don't try to keep these lines straight.
Work with the curve of the gourd.

FLORAL RHAPSODY

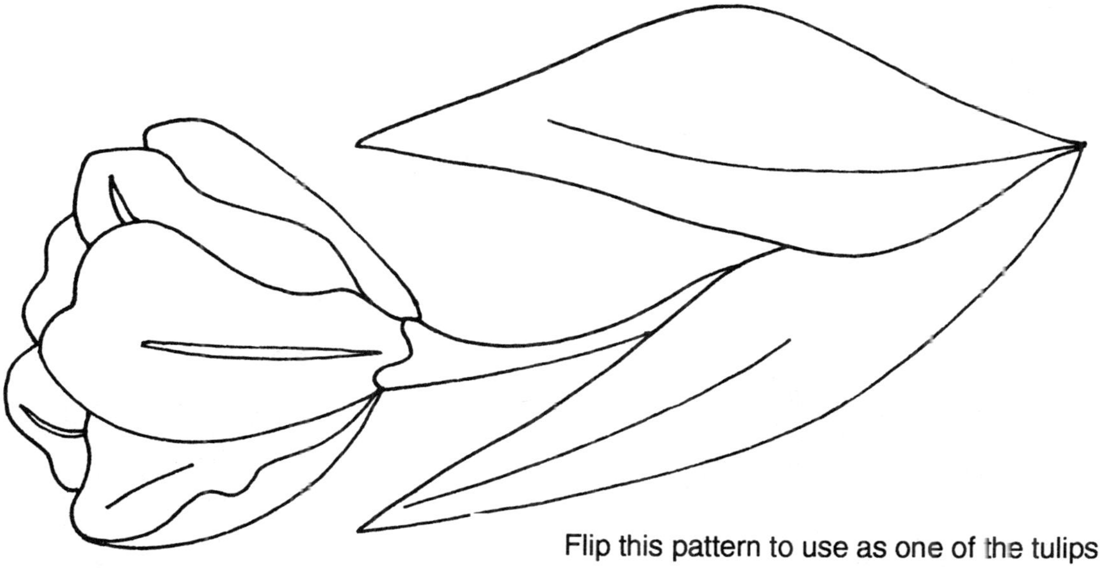

19

Flip this pattern to use as one of the tulips again

POSITION AROUND GOURD, TWO TULIPS FACING EACH OTHER ON EACH SIDE. SPACE ACCORDINGLY.

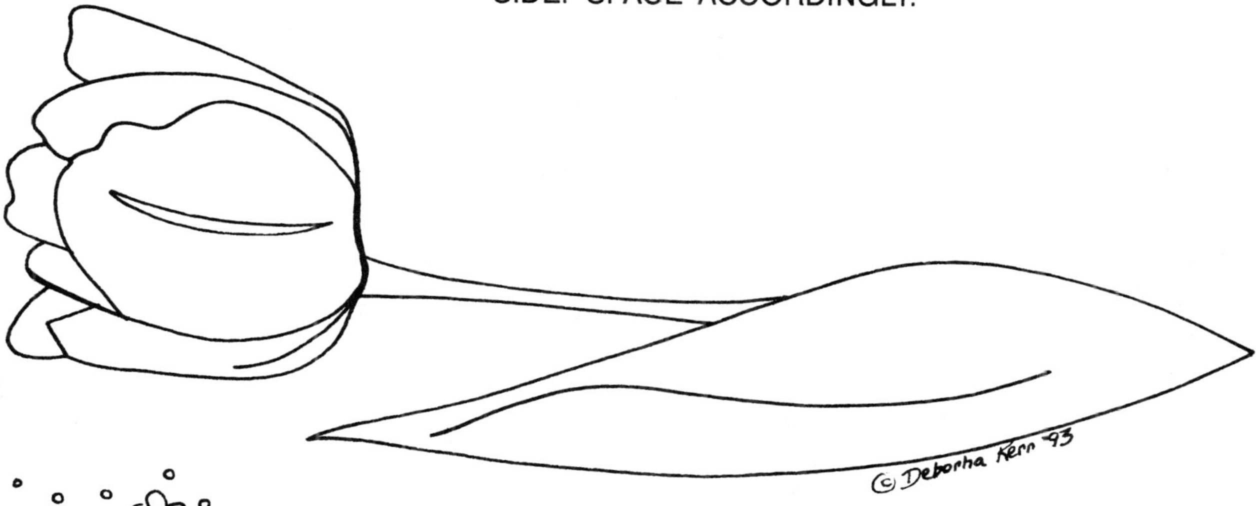

© Deborha Kern '93

Example of Forget Me Nots

Use picture for composition placement.

MOON SKIES

MOON SKIES

PALETTE
Deco Art Americana
Moon Yellow
Taffy Cream
Antique Gold
Burnt Orange
Dark Chocolate
Deco Art Hot Shots
Scorching Yellow
Torrid Orange
Deco Art Heavy Metal
Gold Glitter (Karat Gold)
Folk Art Metallic
Amethyst
Delta Ceramcoat
Laguna
Vintage Wine
Colonial Blue
Folk Art
Baby Blue

1. Basecoat gourd or potbelly with Amethyst. This will take three to four coats for good coverage.
2. Use a sea sponge that has been moistened and squeezed out to apply Laguna then Baby Blue, Vintage Wine and lastly Colonial Blue. Let each color dry before applying the next one.
3. Basecoat moon with Moon Yellow. Float Vintage Wine around outside of moon. Basecoat moon with two more coats of Moon Yellow.
4. Float shading on moon with Burnt Orange. Highlight the right side of moon with Taffy Cream. The eyelashes are liner strokes of Dark Chocolate. Glaze Scorching Yellow over all but Taffy Cream highlight area. Float Torrid Orange over left side of moon.
5. Cut stars from compressed sponge. Dip in water and squeeze. Dip in Antique Gold. Blot off excess paint. Sponge all over gourd applying even pressure.
6. Brush Glitter (gold) over entire gourd except moon. Let dry well and spray varnish.

DECORATIVE HEART STAND
To accompany woven tie birdhouse

PALETTE
Accent Country Colors
Liberty Blue
Deep Forest Green
Folk Art
Raspberry Wine
Delta Ceramcoat
Burnt Umber

1. Sand and seal stand with MinWax Early American. I took the heart base off to make this easier. Sand again lightly.
2. Basecoat heart with Raspberry Wine. Basecoat the top of each decorative round with Liberty Blue then Raspberry Wine then Deep Forest Green. Use a flat brush to keep sharp edges. Have dampened rag handy to wipe off oops.
3. Use Burnt Umber oil paint to antique above and below each decorative round. Rub well first with Blending and Glazing Medium. Use a soft cloth to blend. Also antique sides and around edges of heart. Remove excess with thinner if necessary. Let cure one to two days. Spray varnish.
4. Spatter stand with Burnt Umber. Let dry well. Attach heart base and apply several coats of varnish.

WOVEN TIE BIRDHOUSE

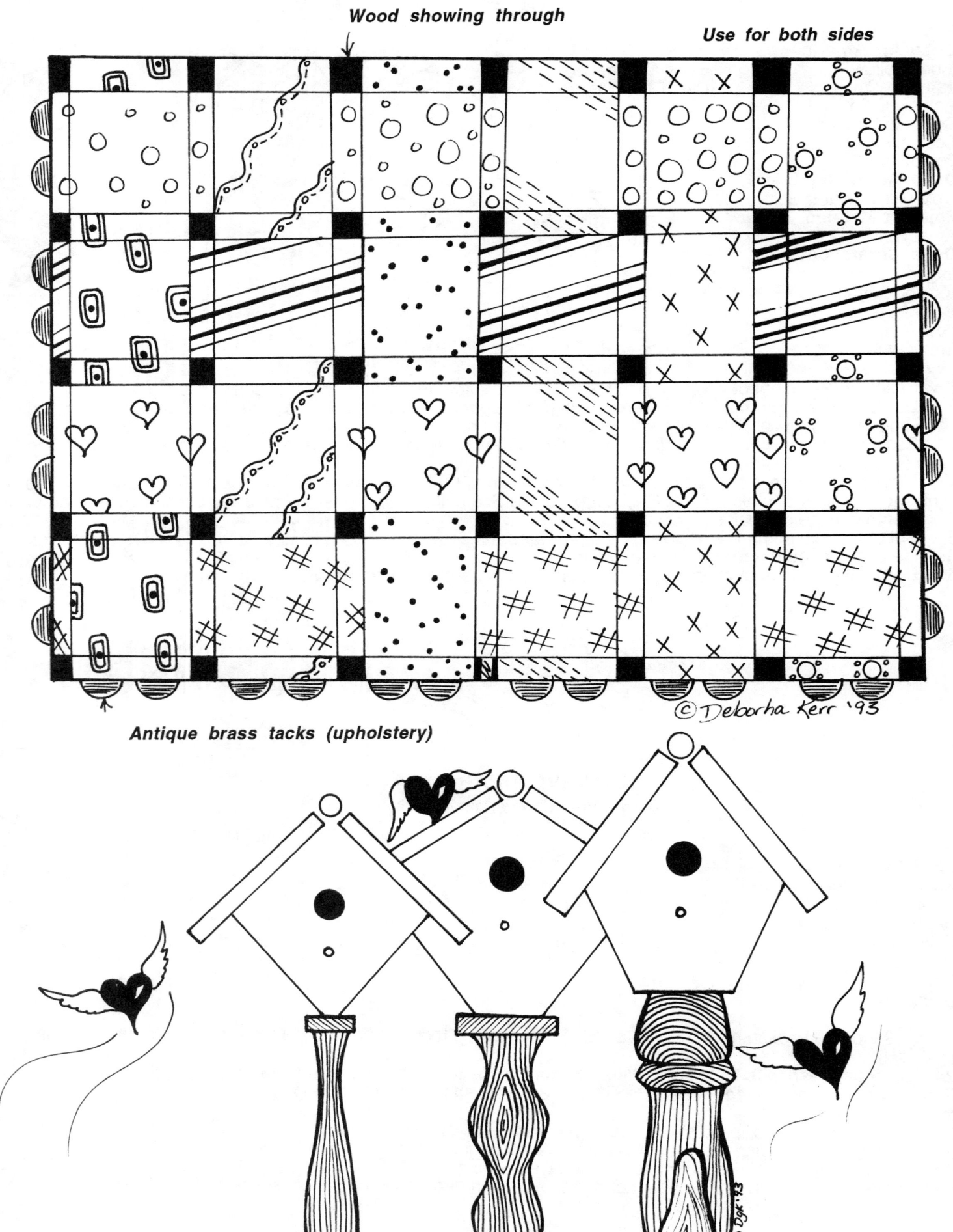

Wood showing through

Use for both sides

Antique brass tacks (upholstery)

© Deborha Kerr '93

WOVEN TIE BIRDHOUSE

PALETTE
Delta Ceramcoat
Candy Bar
Forest Green
Burnt
Deco Art Americana
Antique Gold
Folk Art
Raspberry Wine
Accent Country Colors
Liberty Blue
Deep Forest Green
Raw Umber
Deco Art Hot Shots
Electric Blue
Fiery Red
Thermal Green

Black Green
Light Ivory

I designed this especially to go with the woven tie chair.

1. Sand birdhouse. Seal with MinWax Early American stain. Sand again lightly. Transfer on design. I used Scotch Magic tape for all straight lines.
2. Basecoat all vertical rows first.
   a) Raspberry Wine
   b) Deep Forest Green
   c) Liberty Blue
   d) Raspberry Wine
   e) Deep Forest Green
   f) Liberty Blue
3. Basecoat all horizontal rows.
   a) Liberty Blue
   b) Raspberry Wine
   c) Deep Forest Green
   d) Liberty Blue
4. Do both sides of birdhouse when applying rows. Don't forget over the edges as well.
5. Basecoat base of birdhouse Liberty Blue.
6. Horizontal Rows Designs (both side)
   a) Use the wooden end of a liner brush dipped in Light Ivory.
   b) Basecoat stripes Light Ivory. Use Antique Gold for thin stripes.
   c) Raspberry Wine hearts
   d) Antique Gold crosshatches
7. Vertical Rows Design (both sides)
   a) Antique Gold dots, stylus dots are Forest Green
   b) Light Ivory "X's".
   c) Burnt Umber stylus dots.
   d) Forest Green squiggle lines Antique Gold stylus dot.
   e) Light Ivory rectangles Raspberry Wine stylus dot.
8. Shade outside all Raspberry Wine rows with Candy Bar to establish squares.
9. Shade outside all Liberty Blue rows with Raw Umber to establish squares.
10. Shade outside all Deep Forest Green rows with Black Green to establish squares.
11. Float inside all top squares:
    Raspberry Wine - float with Fiery Red
    Liberty Blue - float with Electric Blue
    Deep Forest Green - Float with Thermal Green
12. Let dry overnight. Varnish lightly with Blair Satin Tole. Apply Burnt Umber oil paint with soft cloth to antique birdhouse. I antiqued around hole under roof line, and on very top of birdhouse.
13. Mist lightly with varnish. Speckle using Burnt Umber. Let dry. Varnish. Lightly hammer two antique brass tacks per tie all around edges of birdhouse.
14. Glue to decorative heart stand.

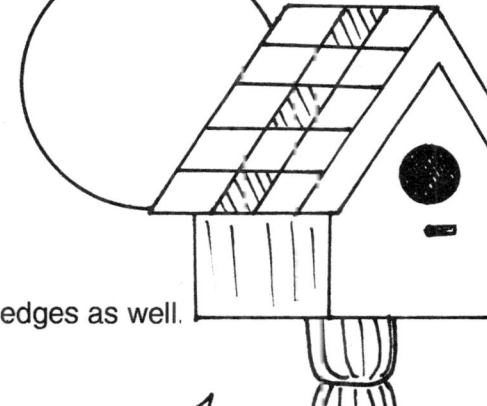

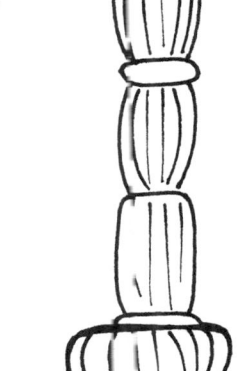

HEAVENS ABOVE

HEAVENS ABOVE

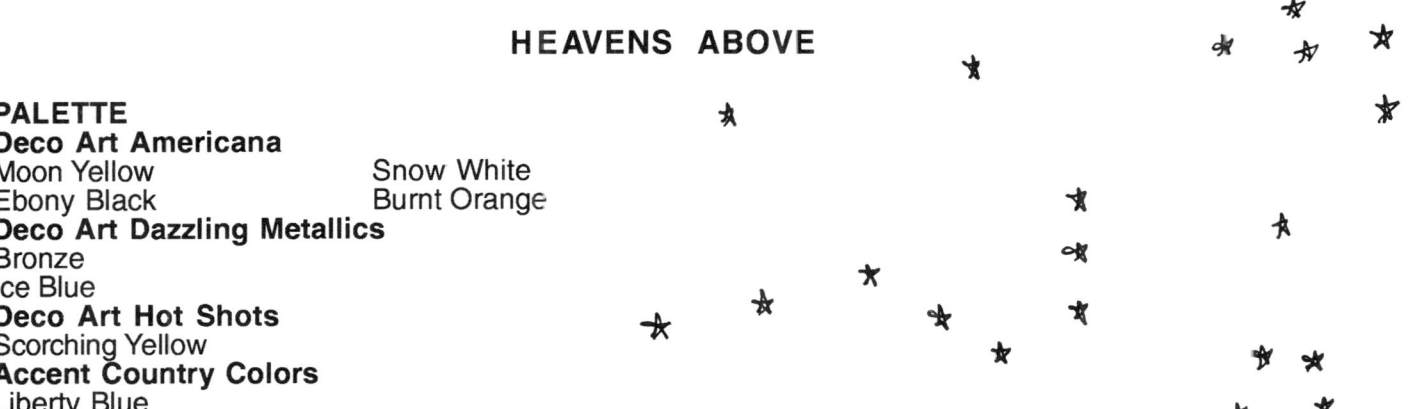

PALETTE
Deco Art Americana
Moon Yellow   Snow White
Ebony Black   Burnt Orange
Deco Art Dazzling Metallics
Bronze
Ice Blue
Deco Art Hot Shots
Scorching Yellow
Accent Country Colors
Liberty Blue
Delta Dazzlers
Frost Stars

1. Basecoat gourd or potbelly 1:1 Ice Blue plus Liberty Blue.
2. Basecoat moon with Moon Yellow. Float shading with Burnt Orange. Linework is Burnt Orange as well on face of moon.
3. Float a light glaze of Bronze over Burnt Orange shading. Highlight with Scorching Yellow. Make dots on moon ends with Bronze.
4. Stars are linework with thinned Snow White. Centers of stars are the end of paint brush dots. Let dry well.
5. Float shading behind moon with Ebony Black
6. Brush Frost Stars over all except the moon.
7. Spray varnish to finish.

WOVEN TIE CHAIR

Looking for something unusual to pass down the family generations? This eclectic tie chair is just the thing for you!

PALETTE
Accent Country Colors
Liberty Blue
Deep Forest Green
Folk Art
Raspberry Wine
Delta Ceramcoat
Burnt Umber

1. Strip and sand chair if necessary. Seal with MinWax Early American stain. Paint second to top round areas with Liberty Blue. Middle areas are Raspberry Wine and bottom areas are Deep Forest Green.
2. Paint top rung Raspberry Wine, middle rung Deep Forest Green and lower rung Liberty Blue. Bottom rung is left Early American.
3. Bottom leg rounded areas are split in three. Top part is Liberty Blue, middle part is Raspberry Wine and lower part is Deep Forest Green. Repeat on all eight areas.
4. Use Burnt Umber oil paint to antique top of each rung and above and below each rounded area. Use a soft rag to blend. Remove with thinner what you do not want.
5. Spatter chair with Burnt Umber. Let dry well and spray with several coats of varnish.
6. You are now ready to do the base of the chair seat. You will need approximately 16 mens' ties in desired colors. Check your local thrift stores for best selections. Keep in mind that you **do not** want stretchy ties.
    I applied Scotch Guard fabric protectant to the ties for better durability. Check for color fastness.
7. Use a staple gun or upholstery tacks to secure row of ties in one direction. Pull quite tight. Ends are tucked underneath the chair. Remember you are using the narrow ends of the ties. Try to have somewhat consistent widths. Weave ties back through in the other direction for second row. Check before you secure for weaving mistakes.
8. Carefully hammer in upholstery tacks along front, back and sides in neat straight lines. I used antique finish brass tacks. Your chair is now ready to admire and enjoy!

For all you "Southwestern" fans!

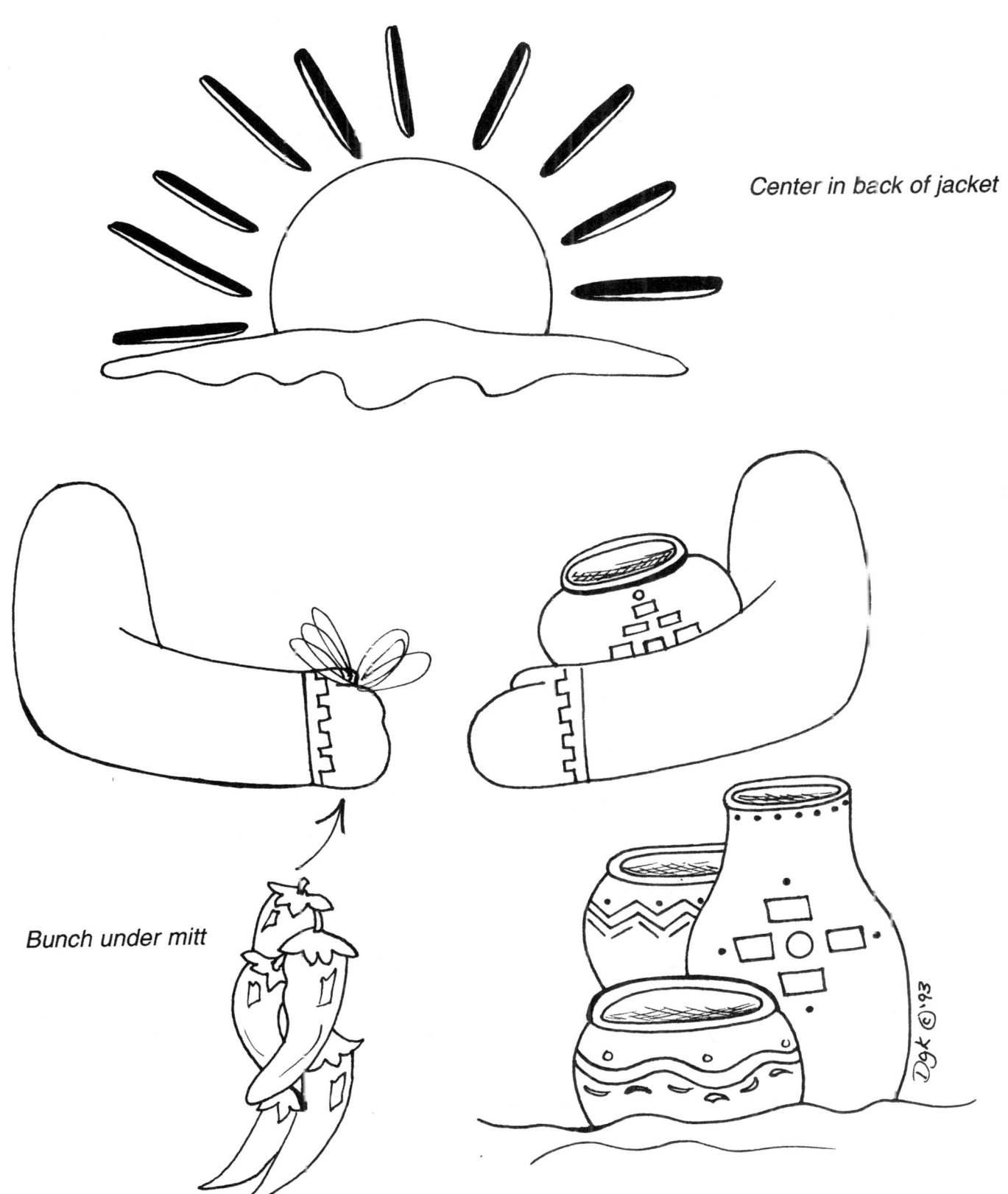

Center in back of jacket

Bunch under mitt

CACTUS CLAUS

PALETTE
Deco Art Americana
Terra Cotta
Snow White
Leaf Green
Medium Flesh
Burnt Orange
Dark Chocolate
Ebony Black
Antique Gold
Country Red
Deco Art Hot Shots
Torrid Orange
Delta Ceramcoat
Laguna
Candy Bar
Adobe
Gamal Green
Hippo Grey
Fleshtone
Avocado
Red Iron Oxide
Burnt Sienna
Colonial Blue
Antique White
Golden Brown
Quaker Grey
Avalon
Yellow
Accent Country Colors
Raw Umber
Folk Art
Baby Blue
Granite Stone
Pueblo Sand

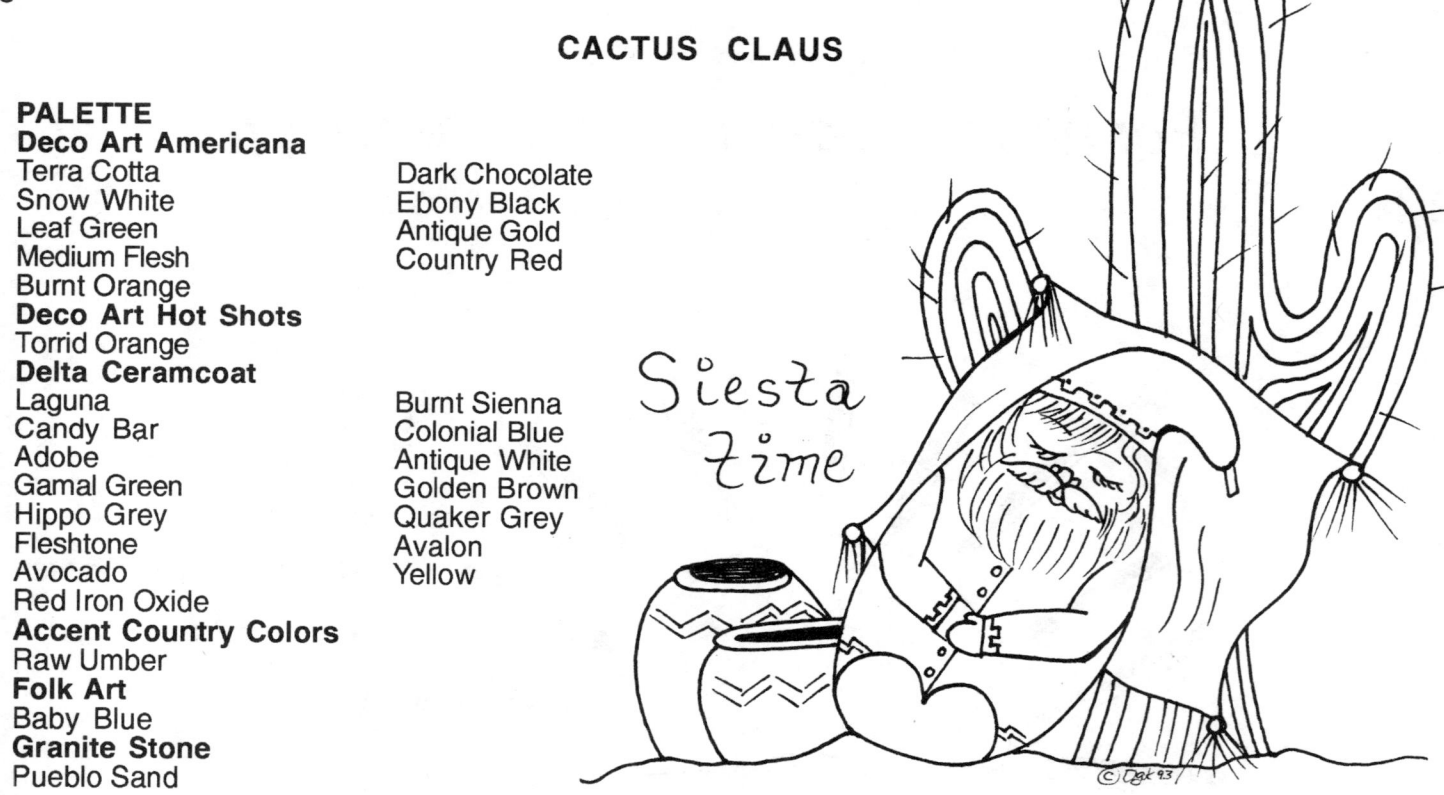

1. Basecoat gourd or potbelly Terra Cotta. Draw a chalk line to indicate hat. Basecoat hat with Laguna. Basecoat feet Dark Chocolate. Lightly transfer on design.
2. Paint face, hair and beard. Float a Burnt Sienna wash around hairline to give a deeper complexion effect. Eyes are Colonial Blue floated with Avalon. Cheeks are an Adobe wash.
3. Basecoat mitts with Antique White. Float shading with Dark Chocolate. Design on mitts is Laguna. Highlight with Snow White.
4. Basecoat buttons with Antique White. Cacti are Avocado. Spikes and details are Dark Chocolate. Use to outline cacti and buttons as well.
5. Basecoat pots with Antique White. Add designs using Country Red and Leaf Green. Float shading with Dark Chocolate. Highlight with Snow White. Stipple on Snow White as well to add some texture. Rims are Dark Chocolate. Outline pots with it as well.
6. Basecoat chili peppers with Country Red. Float shading with Candy Bar. Highlights are Torrid Orange. Drybrush on Snow White shine areas. Chili pepper tops are Leaf Green, shaded and outlined with Gamal Green. Highlight with Thermal Green. Raffia is liner strokes of Golden Brown, Antique White and Antique Gold. Keep thin and wispy looking.
7. Float shading on base of hat above hairline with Avalon. Trim is Antique White with Antique Gold stylus dots.
8. Marking on feet are Antique Gold.
9. Base sun on back of jacket with Burnt Orange. Float at the base with Red Iron Oxide. Brush over with a Yellow wash. The rays are Burnt Orange and Yellow liner strokes. Outline sun with Yellow as well. Basecoat cloud beneath sun with Laguna. Shade with Avalon. Highlight with Baby Blue.
10. Float all shading on jacket above feet, around and inside arm area (except for forearms), to the right of center line of jacket, under hair and beard and around pots and chili peppers. Float highlights with Golden Brown on forearms and to the left of center line of jacket.
11. Apply trim to base of jacket with Antique White. Stylus dots are Country Red.
12. Apply Pueblo Sand Granite Stone with spatula to feet area. Bring some up to base of pots. Let dry well and spray varnish.

SHOWCASE GLASS BRICKS

1. Purchase a glass brick from your local hardware store. These come in various sizes and textures. Take your pick. Use a mirror glass cutter (following the manufacturer's directions), to cut a rectangle opening out of the top.

2. Fill with your favorite small collectibles. I've filled mine with tiny seashells. Other ideas include potpourri, colored sands, marbles, beads, seeds, dried flowers, buttons, etc.

3. These filled bricks would look wonderful staggered throughout a glass brick partition.

FROSTY BLUES

PALETTE
Deco Art Americana
Uniform Blue
Williamsburg Blue
Snow White
Ebony Black
Delta Ceramcoat
Fleshtone
Rouge
Quaker Grey
Candy Bar
Wedgewood Blue
Burnt Sienna
Accent Country Colors
Raw Umber
Deco Art Heavy Metals
Glimmer (clear)

1. Basecoat gourd or potbelly with Snow White. This will take several coats. Basecoat feet with Uniform Blue. Float a soft arc on each foot with Wedgewood Blue. Lightly transfer on design.
2. Paint face, hair and beard. You may omit Hippo Grey in this instance. This will make the hair and beard appear softer looking. Eyes are Wedgewood Blue floated with Williamsburg Blue and outlined with Uniform Blue. Cheeks are a Rouge wash. Add Snow White twinkle stars to eyes.
3. Heart designs are based Wedgewood Blue. Float and outline with Uniform Blue.
4. Basecoat mitts with Uniform Blue. Float with Wedgewood Blue.
5. Float Williamsburg Blue under hairline and beard, around and inside sleeves (except for upper forearms), above feet and above and below snow trim areas. Keep this soft looking. Use a mop brush to blend.
6. Tint the beard and hair with a light Wedgewood Blue wash.
7. Apply Snow Tex to top of hat, cuffs and base of jacket. When well dried brush with Glimmer Clear.
8. Spray with varnish to finish.

CHINA MOSAIC MIRRORS

Wondering what to do with that cracked china cup.....look no more!

Choose china or stoneware of your preference. Small plates work well because they have more pattern per piece.

Wear Protective eyewear. Place china in a doubled plastic bag. Smash lightly with hammer. Do not smash too hard or you will have a bag of powder.

This is somewhat like building a puzzle. Working in small areas at a time glue pieces of china to mirror. Use a good quality white glue. Fit pieces together as tightly as you can. Let dry well.

Apply grout to small area. Let dry partially and while still somewhat soft, scrape grout off china. I found a small fingernail file works well. This is somewhat slow going so do not grout a large area or it will set up too hard and be difficult to scrape off china.

Suggestions:
Collect cracked china that loved ones have held on to. This will make your mirror an extra special keepsake.

Try colored grout for unusual and flattering effects.

Make a mirror featuring your china pattern for a designer look.

ANTIQUE BOBBIN CANDLESTICKS

1. Group together old bobbins found in many antique store.

2. If desired add hearts and dots to the top rims of the bobbins. To make the hearts use the other end of your paint brush and make two dots side by side. Use your stylus to pull down a tail and join the dots.

3. I also like to brush the bobbins with JoSonja Rich Gold mixed with water. This creates a soft glow to the wood - very pretty. Spray varnish.

4. Wrap the bobbins with interesting, nubby yarns. Use lots of yarn - don't be stingy. It is far more effective. Add long, tapered candlesq and you have a wonderful grouping.

FROSTY BLUES

32 FROSTED FOREST

FROSTED FOREST

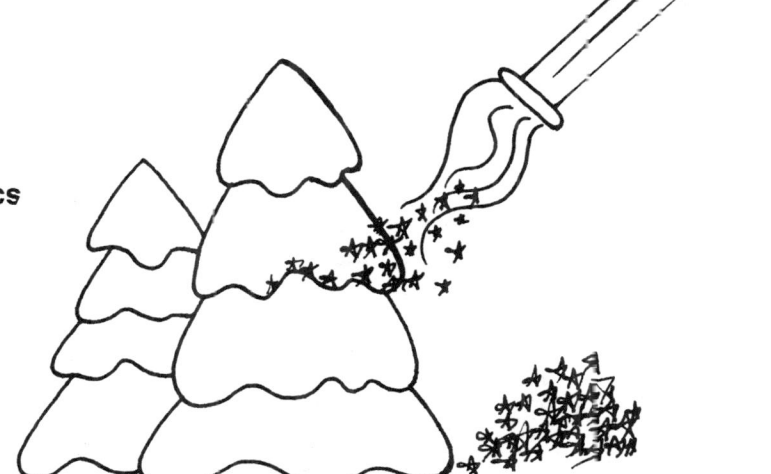

PALETTE
Deco Art Americana
Williamsburg Green
Snow White
Ultra Blue Deep
Deco Art Dazzling Metallics
Crystal Green
Glorious Gold
Deco Art Heavy Metals
Glimmer (Clear)
Delta Ceramcoat
Deep River
Quaker Grey
Antique White
Black Green
Accent Country Colors
Deep Forest Green

1. Sand and seal wooden plate with Jo Sonja All Purpose Sealer. Sand again lightly.
2. Basecoat plate with Williamsburg Blue. Lightly transfer on design.
3. Basecoat trees left to right: Deep River, Crystal Green and Deep Forest Green. Float tree divisions with Antique White and Black Green. Use Deep Forest Green for center tree. Outline trees with Black Green.
4. Basecoat star Glorious Gold. Apply rays.
5. Basecoat the bottom area of trees with Quaker Grey.
6. Float and walk out Snow White on left side of inside edge of plate. This may take two to three layers.
7. Float and walk out Ultra Blue Deep on right side of inside edge of plate. This may take two to three layers.
8. Add Snow White glass highlights.
9. Using a dry deerfoot stippler and Snow White pounce over entire plate including outside rim. Make this very frosty and snowy looking.
10. Brush over entire plate surface with Glimmer Clear. This adds a wonderful snow sparkle quality. Let dry and spray varnish.

PALETTE
Accent Country Colors
Deep Forest Green

I found this lamp in an antique store. It was such a great idea I wanted to share with you.

1. You will need a thin cylindrical lamp. Cut sticks of approximate same size and length to go around your lamp.

2. Cut a piece of wood in a circle. The circle should be large enough to allow a 1" overhang after the sticks are applied to the cylinder. Stain circle or paint desired color. The edge may be routered if desired. Glue or screw to bottom of lamp.

3. Use a hot glue gun and attach sticks one by one to the lamp cylinder and each other until completely covered. This will take a few layers of sticks.

4. Braid natural raffia. Wrap around sticks at top, center and bottom. Attach with glue gun.

5. Pick a lamp shade of your choice. I chose a grass cloth shade. Cut compressed sponge to pattern size heart. Dip in water and squeeze out. Mix two parts Deep Forest Green and one part Fabric Painting Medium. Load sponge in paint taking care to blot off excess. Apply carefully to pre-marked chalk marks. Make sure to apply even pressure. To cure paint simply put shade back on your lamp and turn it on for a couple of hours!

6. Glue trim or ribbon of your choice around top and bottom of shade.

NATURE'S DIVERSITY

NATURE'S DIVERSITY

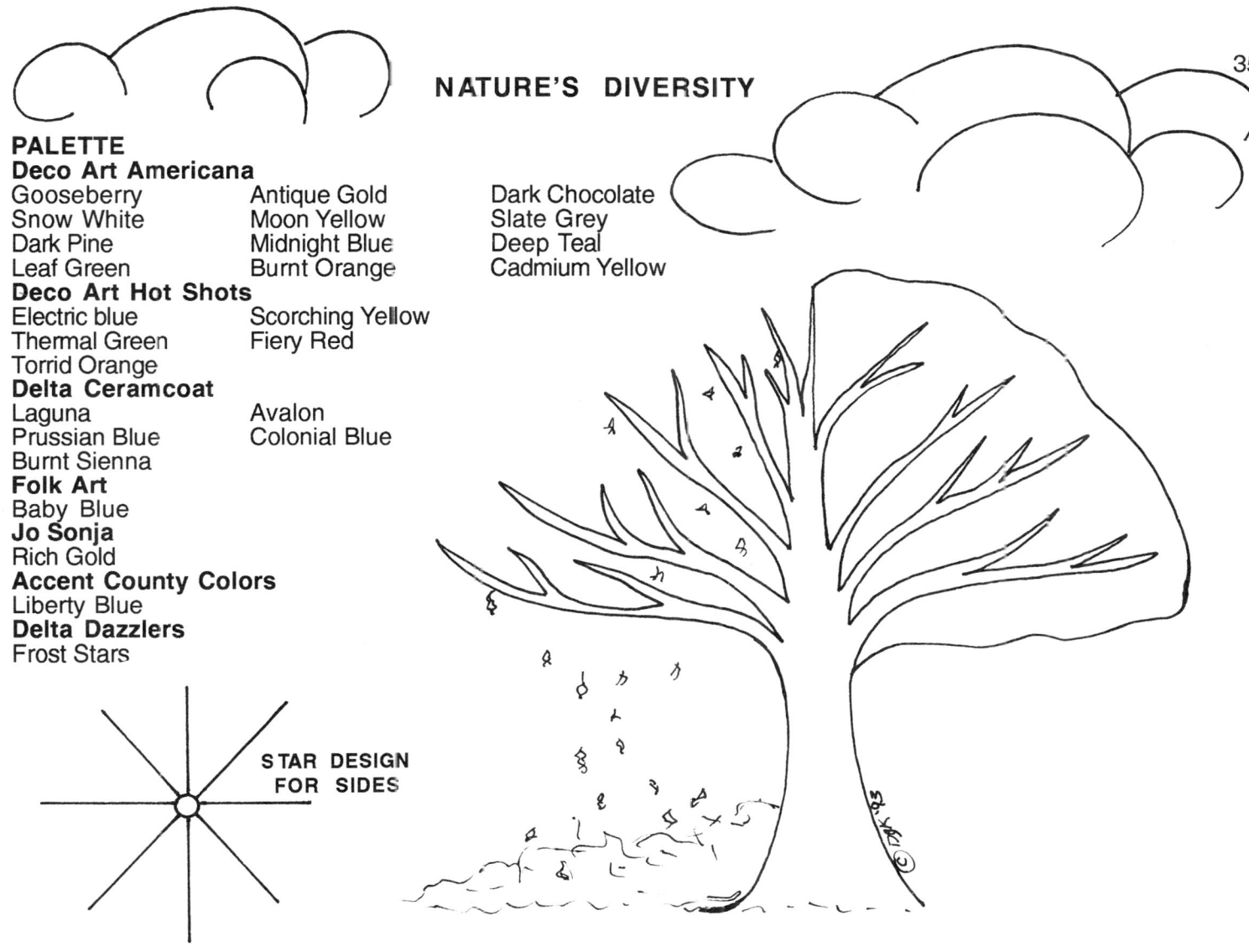

PALETTE
Deco Art Americana
Gooseberry
Snow White
Dark Pine
Leaf Green
Antique Gold
Moon Yellow
Midnight Blue
Burnt Orange
Dark Chocolate
Slate Grey
Deep Teal
Cadmium Yellow

Deco Art Hot Shots
Electric blue
Thermal Green
Torrid Orange
Scorching Yellow
Fiery Red

Delta Ceramcoat
Laguna
Prussian Blue
Burnt Sienna
Avalon
Colonial Blue

Folk Art
Baby Blue

Jo Sonja
Rich Gold

Accent County Colors
Liberty Blue

Delta Dazzlers
Frost Stars

1. Sand and seal planter with Jo Sonja All Purpose Sealer. Sand again light.
2. Basecoat inside and ends with Liberty Blue.
3. Basecoat side of planter with Baby Blue. Basecoat trim and inside heart cutouts with Antique Gold and then Rich Gold. Streak left half of front side with Laguna then less Avalon, then less Prussian Blue. Streak Colonial Blue over all. Use a wide flat brush and have the planter slightly moistened. Do same over entire back side of planter.
4. Streak Gooseberry then Cadmium Yellow on right front side of planter.
5. Lightly transfer on pattern, avoiding details. Basecoat Wind with Slate Grey. Float shading with Williamsburg Blue. Highlight with Snow White + a dab of Slate Grey. Glaze Slate Grey areas with Electric Blue. Keep Wind patterns soft and hazy looking. Float shading below and behind Wind with Midnight Blue. This may take two layers. Float in some Snow White hazy lines to the right of Wind.
6. Basecoat Sun with Moon Yellow. Float shading with Burnt Orange. Add tints of Torrid Orange and Scorching Yellow. Sun's eye is Antique Gold. Outline and fill in pupil with Dark Chocolate. Detail on Sun's face is Burnt Orange. Float to the right of Sun with Burnt Orange.
7. Basecoat tree trunk with Burnt Sienna. Float shading with Dark Chocolate. Float left side of tree trunk with Midnight Blue. Float right side with Torrid Orange. Use a dry deerfoot stippler to apply Teal Green then Dark Pine then Leaf Green foliage to right side of tree. Do not clean brush in between greens. Let dry then stipple in Torrid Orange, Scorching Yellow, Thermal Green and Fiery Red blossoms. Do not overdo this. Stipple in dry leaves at base of tree on left side of trunk with Dark Pine, then Dark Chocolate and Burnt Sienna. Do not clean brush in between. Leaves are mixed combinations of the same colors. They are little liner dabs.
8. Use a liner brush for the starts on the ends of the planter. Use the end of your paint brush for the center dots in each star.
9. Float Snow White clouds over the back of the planter. Keep light and fluffy looking. It may help to have the planter slightly moistened. Use a mop brush for soft blending.
10. When completely dry, brush over ends with Frost Stars. Spray varnish several coats to finish.
11. I then filled the planter with florist foam. Cover that with Spanish Moss. Line the planter with silk flowers of your choice.

GHOST SHELLS

MERMAID MANOR
Pages 46,47,48,49,50,51,52,53

BLOSSOMS
Pages 68, 69

STRAWBERRY NICK
Pages 65, 66, 67

Basecoat Face Medium Flesh.

Lightly transfer on line. Basecoat eyes White.

Basecoat eyes desired color. Float shading with Burnt Sienna.

Float shading on left side of irises. Add Black pupils and White highlights. Outline eyes with Raw Umber. Float wash of desired color on cheeks, under side of nose and bottom lip. Mouth is Candy Bar.

EYE COLOR VARIATIONS

CACTUS CLAUS
Pages 26, 27, 28

PUNCHED TIN AND HOLLYHOCKS
Page 13

LOVEBIRD STOOL
Pages 14, 15

SLEDDIN SANTA
Pages 16, 17

HEAVENS ABOVE
Pages 24, 25

MOON SKIES
Pages 20, 21

GALAXY
Pages 54, 55, 56

NATURES DIVERSITY
Pages 34, 35

GHOST SHELLS

PALETTE
Accent Country Colors
Deep Forest Green
Delta Ceramcoat
Black Green
Folk Art
Teal Green
Hallmark Home Decor
Antiquing Gel - Patina

1. Sand and then seal birdhouse with Jo Sonja All Purpose Sealer.
2. Basecoat with Deep Forest Green. Lightly sand again.
3. Float shells on front and bubbles on sides with Teal Green. Keep these light and "ghostlike" looking. Float shading on shells with Black Green. Let dry well.
4. Using a natural sea sponge that has been dampened and rung out well, apply Antiquing Gel - Patina all over birdhouse. Alternate wrist position so the pattern will keep changing. Make sure to blot excess paint off onto paper towels before applying to birdhouse.
5. Spray varnish to seal.

ABALONE HUT

PALETTE
Accent Country Color
Liberty Blue
Deco Americana
Buttermilk

1. Sand and seal birdhouse with Jo Sonja All Purpose Sealer. Sand again lightly.
2. Basecoat house and perch with Buttermilk. Basecoat roof and inside hole with Liberty Blue.
3. Scrollwork is Liberty Blue.
4. Glue tiny pieces of abalone shell to the roof covering it. Let dry well, and spray with several coats of varnish.

SURF AND SAND

1. Purchase an inexpensive wooden picture frame. Sand lightly. Remove the glass and backing.

2. Paint with a thick coat of Granite Stone Pueblo Sand texture paint. Let dry overnight.

3. Paint on another thick layer. Let the sand build up in layers in a "dune" effect. This will create more visual interest than a flat application. Let dry well. Apply one more coat if necessary.

4. Glue tiny seashells, polished abalone, sand dollars, starfish, etc. around the frame. Leave lots of sand showing through. Let dry well and spray with a couple of coats of varnish. Insert your favorite ocean snapshot and ....
   Voila! a fun way to showcase your beachcombing treasures.

5. Another option is to glue small seashells directly onto the glass of one of your favorite framed photographs.

MERMAID MANOR

SIDE ONE

MERMAID MANOR

PALETTE

Deco Art Americana
Medium Flesh	Yellow Ochre	Antique Gold	Williamsburg Blue
Cadmium Yellow	Gooseberry Pink	Raspberry	Snow White
Dark Chocolate	Burnt Orange	Olive Green	Moon Yellow
Ebony Black			

Deco Art Dazzling Metallics
Bronze, Ice Blue, Shimmering Silver, Crystal Green

Deco Art Heavy Metals
Glimmer (clear)

Deco Art Hot Shots
Scorching Yellow, Torrid Orange, Thermal Green, Fiery Red, Electric Blue

Delta Ceramcoat
Avalon Fleshtone	Light Ivory	Kelly Green	
Old Parchment	Woodland Night	Hippo Grey	Vintage Wine
Dusty Purple	Midnight	Antique White	Spice Tan
Indiana Rose	Green Sea	Tangerine	Rouge
Straw	Jubilee Green	Prussian Blue	Burnt Sienna
Deep River	Blue Mist	Spice Brown	Red Iron Oxide
Quaker Grey	Gamal Green	Lavender	Avocado

Folk Art
Baby Blue, Heather, Lavender Sachet, Butter Pecan

Ceramcoat Gleams
Pinkie Pearl, Pearl Finish

Delta Hallmark Home Decor Antiquing Gel
Patina

Accent County Colors
Raw Umber, Barn Red

Jo Sonja's Artist's Gouache
Rich Gold

Duncan Granite Stone
Pueblo Sand

Jo Sonja Crackle Medium

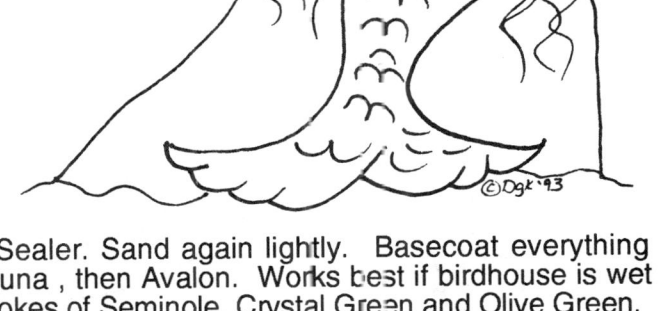

Sand and seal birdhouse with Jo Sonja All Purpose Sealer. Sand again lightly. Basecoat everything except bottom with Baby Blue. Sand lightly. Streak on Laguna, then Avalon. Works best if birdhouse is wet too. Seaweed around bottom of entire birdhouse is brush strokes of Seminole, Crystal Green and Olive Green.

FRONT
1. Basecoat door and inside hole with Midnight.
2. Basecoat mermaid's shell Snow White. Go over with Pearl Finish. Float lines with Hippo Grey. Float Hippo Grey around mermaid's tail.
3. Basecoat pink shell Indiana Rose. Float with Gooseberry Pink. Highlight with Fleshtone. Glaze Gooseberry Pink areas with Pinkie Pearl.
4. Basecoat shell beside pink shell with Blue Mist. Float shading with Heather. Linework is Dusty Purple. Float tints of Baby Blue.
5. Basecoat Kissing Gourami Salem Blue. Float shading with Electric Blue. Highlight with Snow White. Add Electric Blue linework. Eyes are Shimmering Silver. Pupil is Ebony Black. Bubbles are washes of Snow White, keep them transparent. Use a round brush.
6. Basecoat mermaid's skin Medium Flesh. Float shading Burnt Sienna. Cheek is Rouge wash. Eyelash is Raw Umber.
7. Base mermaid's tail Kelly Green. Bottom of tail is Deep River. Float scales with Deep River. Highlight with Thermal Green. Cover all of tail with Glimmer.

8. Basecoat mermaid's hair Red Iron Oxide.
9. Float waves in with Dark Chocolate. Stroke curls in with Barn Red liner marks. Add more liner marks in Tangerine, then Torrid Orange.
10. Basecoat clam shell around hole with four thick coats of Light Ivory. Apply thick coat of Jo Sonja Crackle Medium Let dry. Glaze over with Spice Tan wash. Float Burnt Sienna to separate lines. Top section of shell is thin line of Light Ivory.
11. Basecoat sign post Midnight. Basecoat sign with four thick coats of Barn Red. Add lettering with Raw Umber. Brush thick coat of Jo Sonja Crackle Medium over all. Let dry. Glaze with Rich Gold. Go over lettering if necessary. Attach to sign post with natural jute.

SIDE 1

12. Basecoat porthole Midnight. Outside of porthole is based Burnt Orange. Go over with Bronze . Stipple on Patina. When dry float inner edge of porthole with Baby Blue. Float Burnt Sienna around outer edge. Add lines and stylus dots in Burnt Sienna.
13. Basecoat mermaid's skin Medium Flesh. Face features are sideloads of Burnt Sienna. Cheeks and lips are washes of Rouge. Float under chin and chest area with Burnt Sienna. Highlight nose area with Fleshtone.
   Basecoat eyes Snow White. Irises are Green Sea. Outline with Deep River. Pupils are Ebony Black. Highlight with Snow White. Outline eyes and lashes with Raw Umber.
   Base hair Spice Brown. Float in waves with Old Parchment. Stroke in curls with Old Parchment liner marks. Float with Spice Tan then Spice Brown. Stroke in curls with Antique White.
14. Basecoat mermaid pearls Snow White. Go over with Pearl Finish. Float with Raspberry to separate. Outline with Quaker Grey.
15. Add Snow White highlights to porthole glass. Float Snow White on left side of glass.
16. Basecoat smelts Shimmering Silver. Add details and outline with Ebony Black.
17. Basecoat three fish White. Go over with Cadmium Yellow. Add markings in Crystal Green. Tail and fins are Dusty Purple. Highlight with Scorching Yellow. Add fin markings with Scorching Yellow. Add thick lines of Deep River to top and bottom of fish Eyes are Snow White and Ebony Black.
18. Basecoat starfish Ice Blue. Float with Midnight to separate legs. Midnight is also used to area between front legs. Outline with Midnight on outer edges and Baby Blue on inside area. Add stylus dots with Midnight.
19. Basecoat pod weeds with Avocado. Stems are Gamal Green. Float left side of each pod with Gamal Green. Highlight right sides of pods with Thermal Green.
20. Basecoat crab with Burnt Orange. Float shading with Dark Chocolate to separate legs and face. Brush in glazes of Bronze . Highlight with Torrid Orange. Eyes are Ebony Black. Highlight in eye is Snow White. Basecoat shell Antique White. Float divisions with Spice Tan.
21. Fishing bass are basecoated with washes of Jubilee Green. Keep these transparent looking Float around insides of balls with Gamal Green. Highlight with Thermal Green.

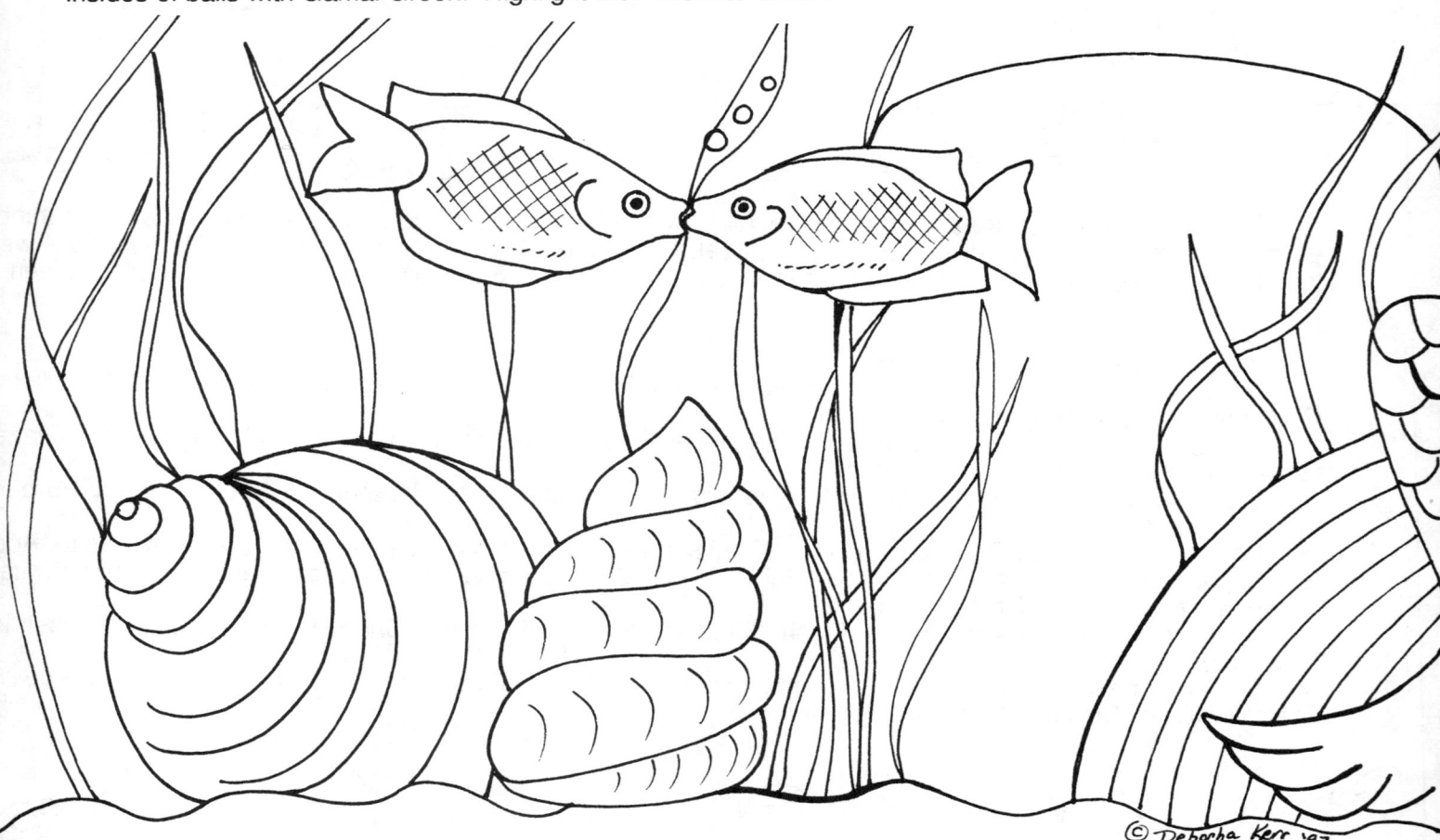

© Deborha Kerr '93

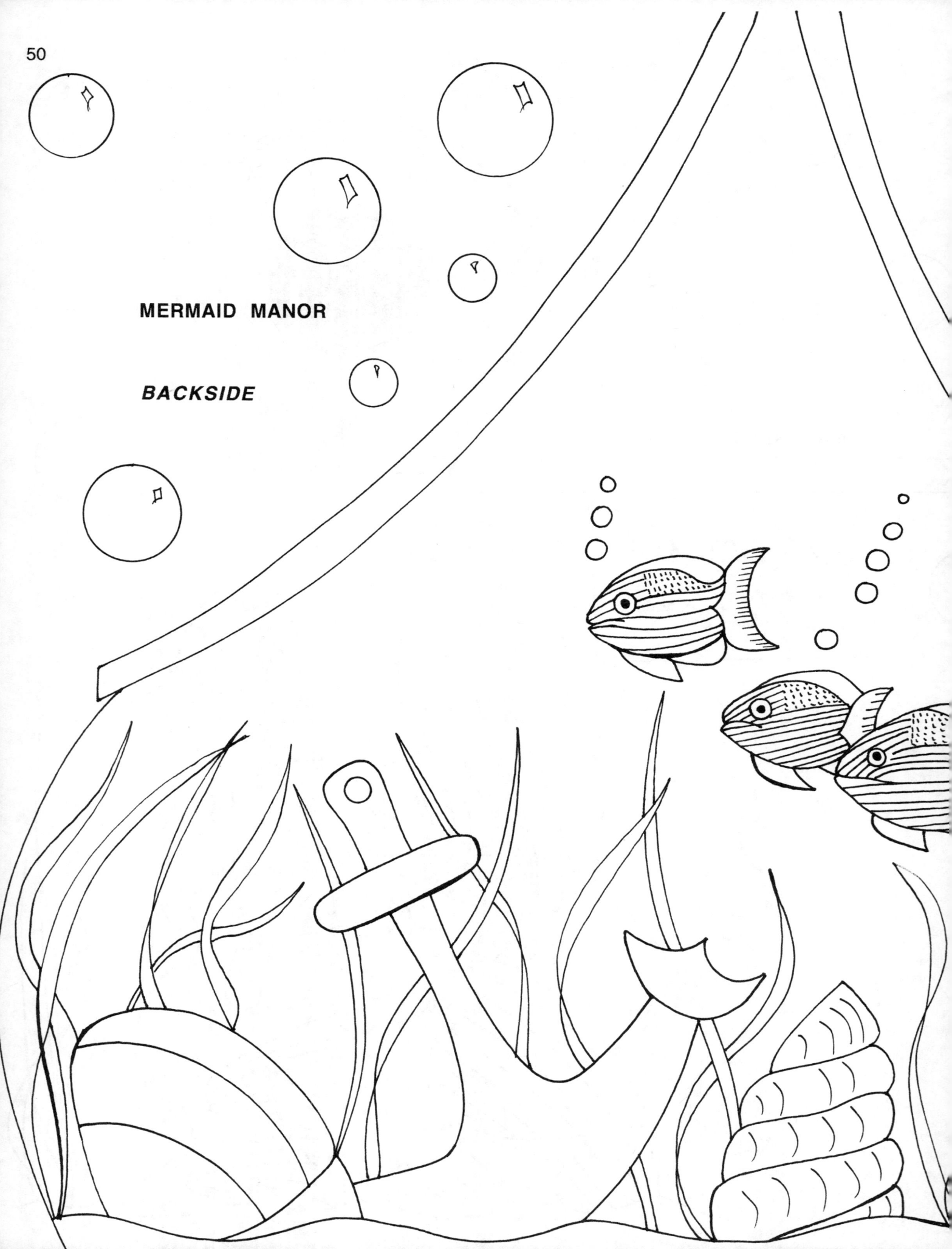

BACK

22. Basecoat anchor Quaker Gray. Shade with Hippo Grey. Highlight with Snow White.
23. Basecoat French Grunts Moon Yellow. Fins are Straw. Float with Cadmium Yellow. Mix tad of Butter Pecan and Black. Use to outline fish and add tail fin markings. Add Salem Blue linework. Float tail fin with Salem Blue. Eyes are Silver. Pupils are Ebony Black. Mouth is Quaker Grey. Bubbles, see #5.
24. Fishing Ball, see #21.
25. Shell by anchor is basecoated with four coats of Light Ivory. Apply thick coat of Jo Sonja Crackle Medium. Let dry. Float lines and around edges of shell with Antique Gold. Highlight with White.
26. Shell, see #4.
27. Basecoat Siamese Fighting Fish Williamsburg Blue. Shade with Prussian Blue. Highlight with Electric Blue. Two front fins and gill are based Burnt Orange then Bronze. Float a side section down center fin Burnt Orange then Bronze as well. Outline and linework with Midnight.

SIDE 2

28. Basecoat seahorse Antique Gold. Float shading with Burnt Sienna. Marking on nose is Burnt Sienna as well. Float some Dark Chocolate here and there down back region for further definition. Basecoat scales Old Parchment. Outline and float around each scale with Antique Gold. Outline stomach area by scales with thin line of Burnt Sienna. Eyes are Ebony Black and Snow White highlight. Bubbles, see #5.
29. Basecoat starfish Dusty Purple. Float shading with Prussian Blue. Highlight with Fiery Red. Add stylus dots in Fiery Red and Prussian Blue.
30. Net is thin lines painted on with Butter Pecan. Outline rope markings with Spice Brown over Butter Pecan. Float edge of net area with Spice Brown.
31. Fishing ball, see #21.

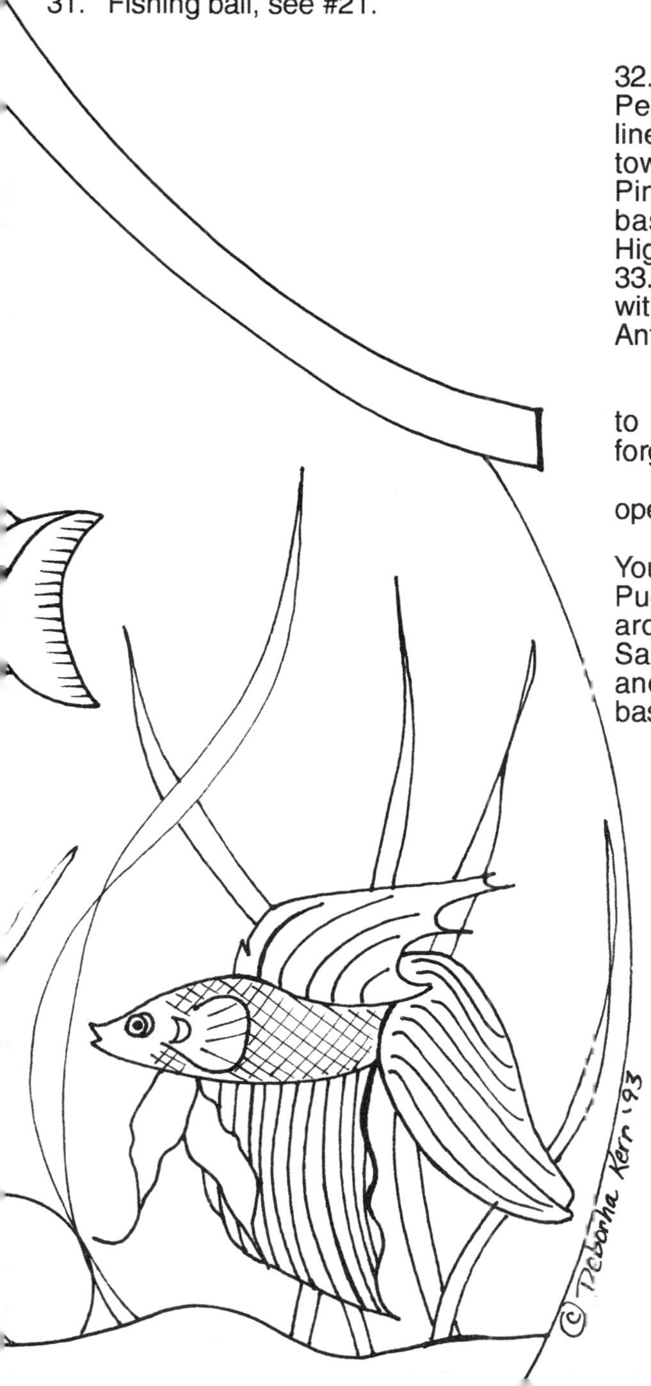

32. Basecoat Snail shell Lavender. Mix Vintage Wine and tad of Pearl Finish. Use to float shading. Walk out fairly wide on center line of shell towards front of of snail. Outline on center line of shell towards front of snail. Outline with Vintage Wine. Highlight with Pinkie Pearl. Add large stylus dots with Vintage Wine. Snail is based Quaker Grey. Shade and outline with Hippo Grey. Highlight with Snow White.
33. Basecoat sand dollar Antique White. Outline inner markings with Antique Gold. Float inside markings with Antique Gold. Float Antique Gold inside outer edge of sand dollar.

Float around everything with Avalon. May take multiple coats to reach desired depths. Make sure you use clean water. Don't forget to float around base of chimney over net area.

Add thin Avalon wash lines over some shells, doorway opening, etc. Keep light and hazy looking.

Apply thick coat of Pueblo Sand to entire base of birdhouse. You will want to remove bottom section if screwed in. Apply Pueblo Sand to bottom of birdhouse under shells, etc., all the way around. Apply in sweeping lines. Let dry. Apply more Pueblo Sand to build up levels and make look more water swept. Apply another thick coat to base painting in opposite direction. Screw base back on and spray varnish to protect.

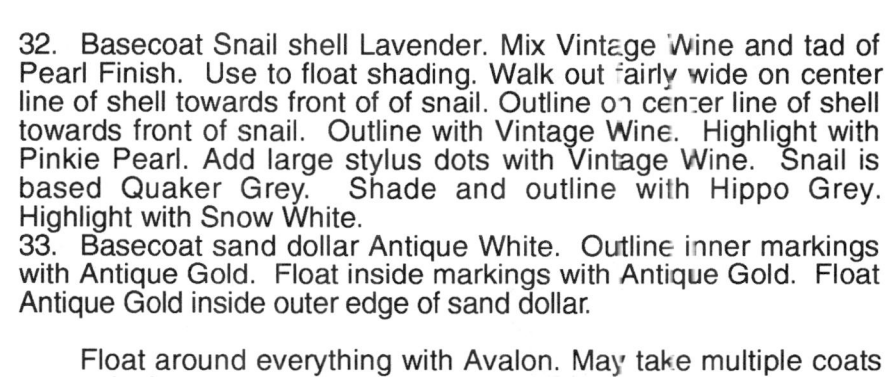

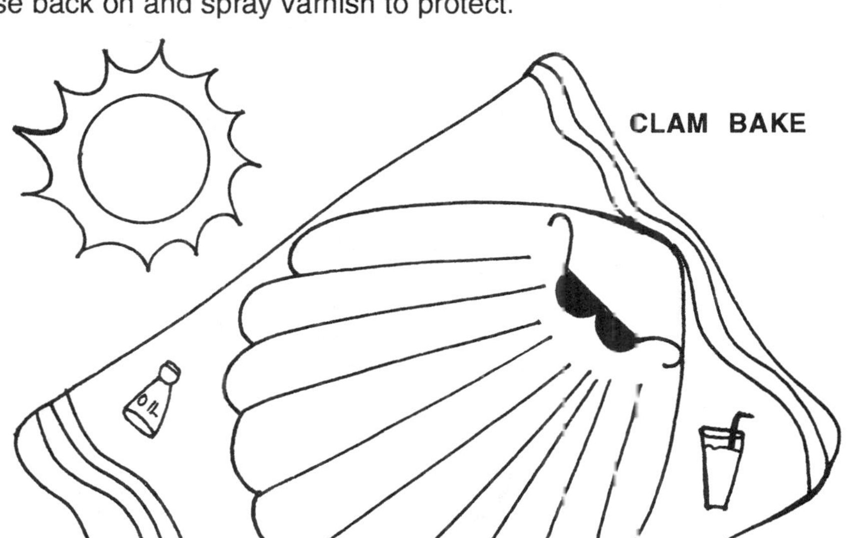

CLAM BAKE

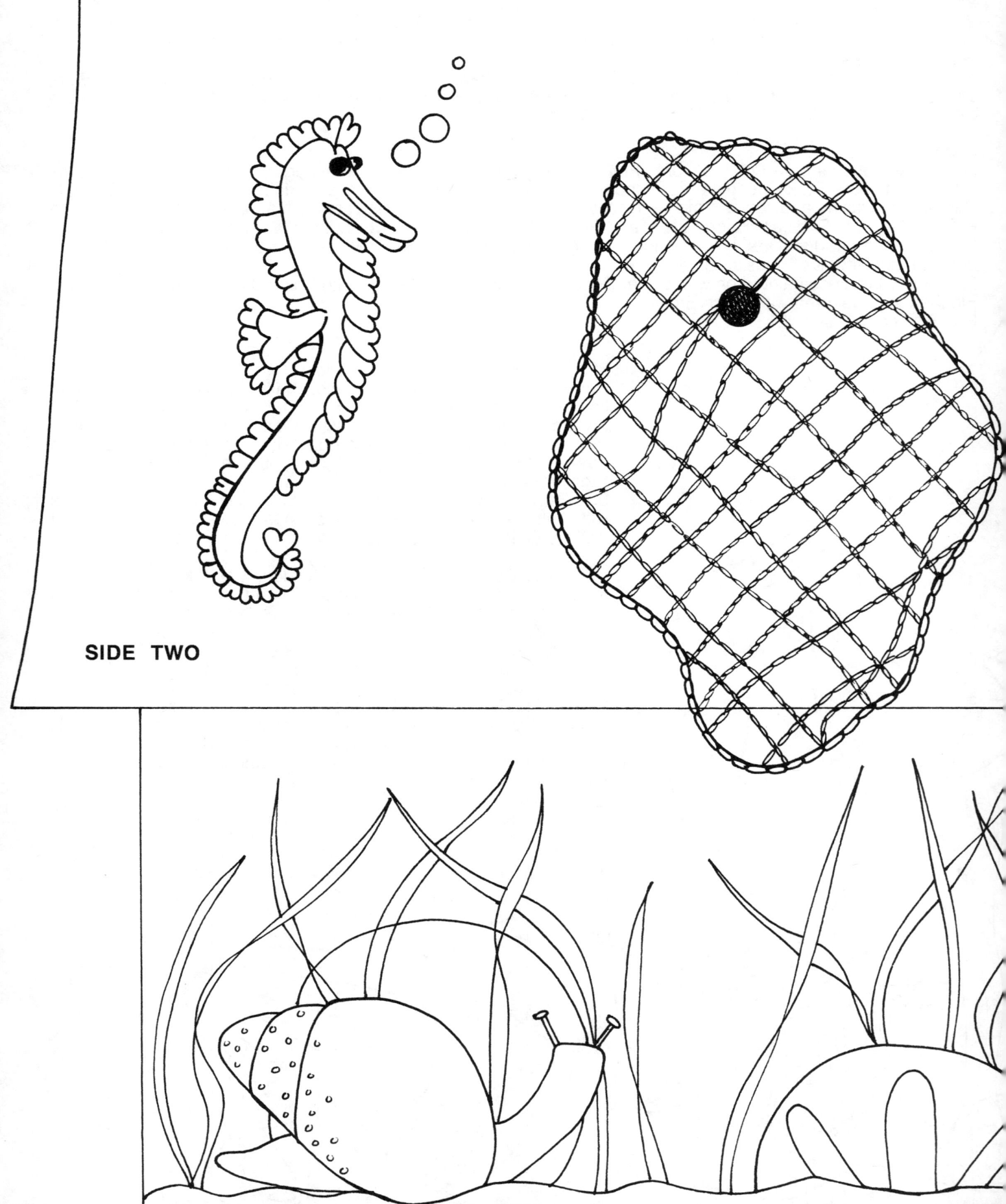

CHIMNEY STACK PROFILES

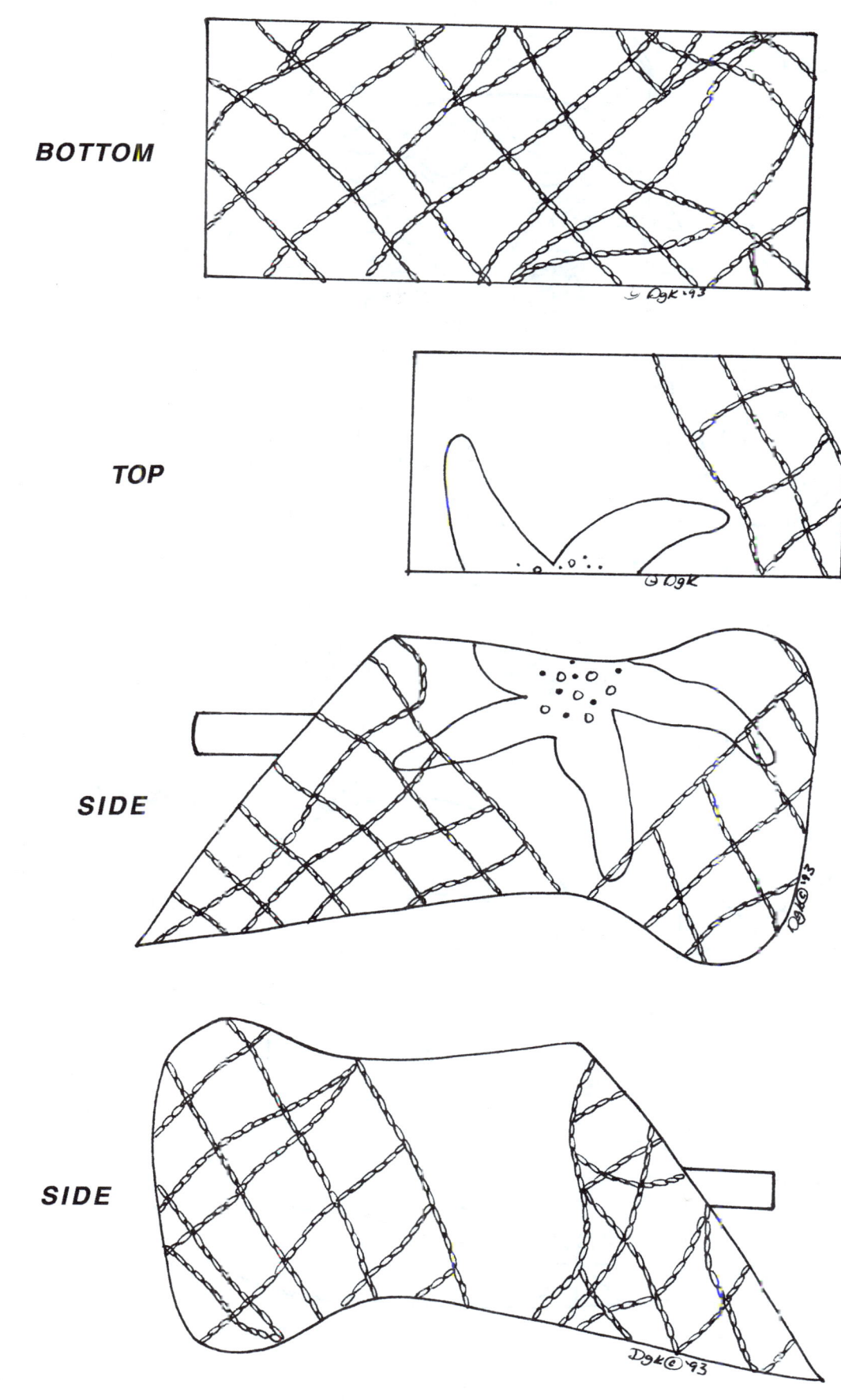

BOTTOM

TOP

SIDE

SIDE

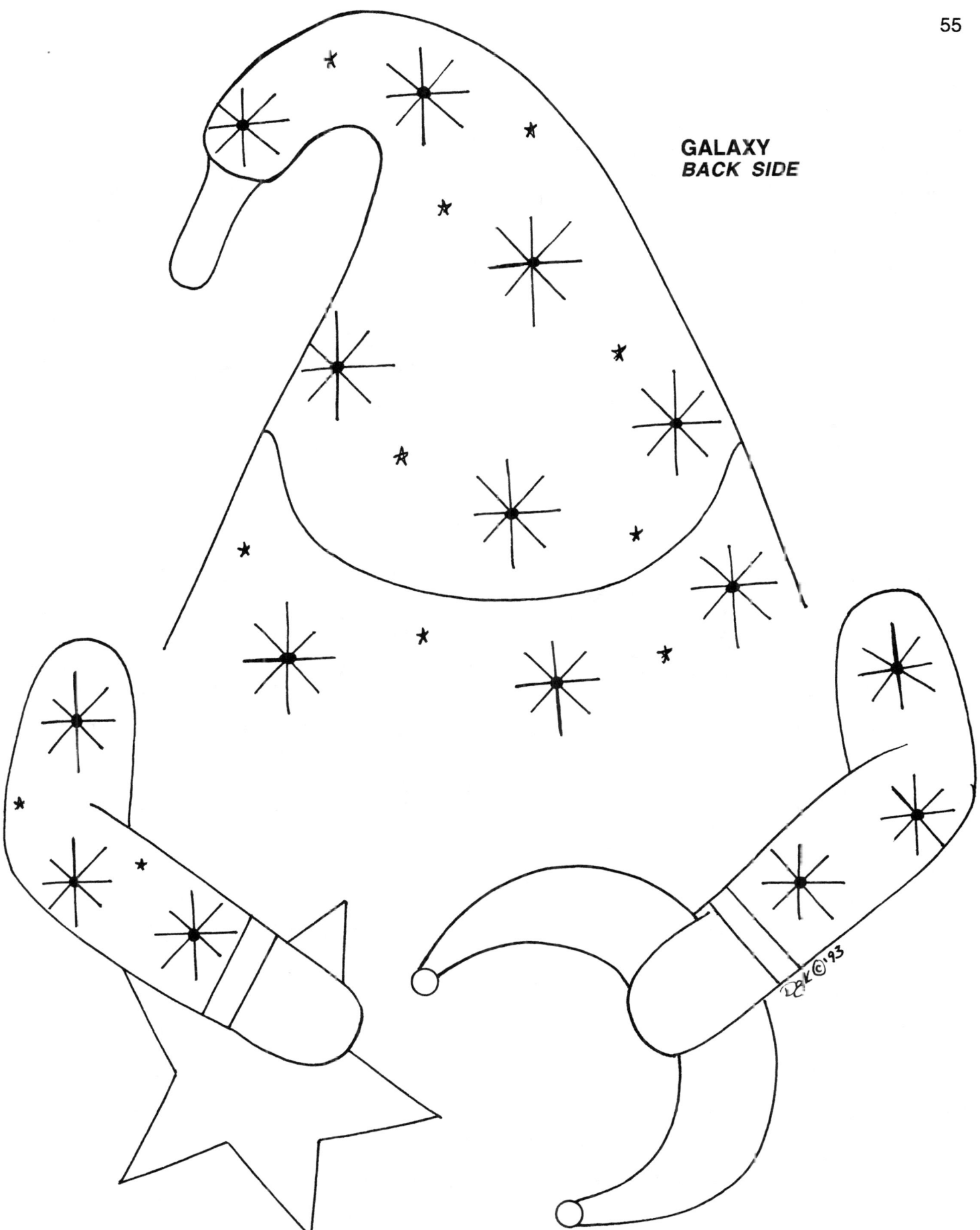
GALAXY
BACK SIDE

GALAXY

PALETTE
Deco Art American
Burnt Orange   Uniform Blue
Ebony Black   Snow White
Moon Yellow   Medium Flesh
Deco Art Hot Shots
Scorching Yellow
Thermal Green
Deco Art Dazzling Metallics
Bronze
Ice Blue
Delta Ceramcoat
Deep River   Green Sea
Fleshtone   Candy Bar
Quaker Grey   Hippo Grey
Rouge   Blue Mist
Avalon   Burnt Sienna
Accent Country Colors
Liberty Blue
Raw Umber
Delta Dazzlers
Frost Stars
Folk Art
Baby Blue

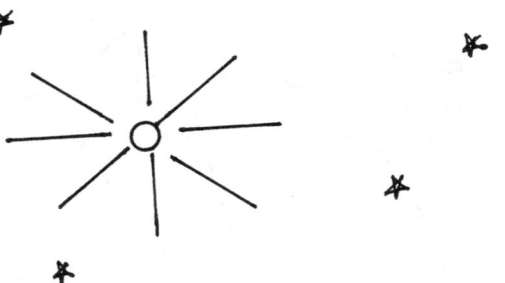

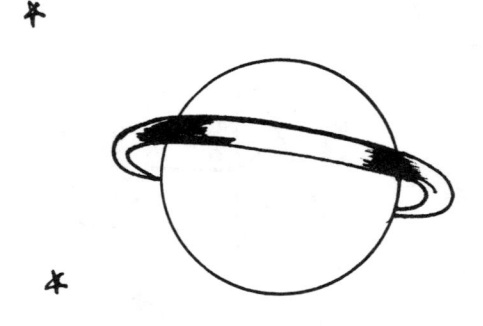
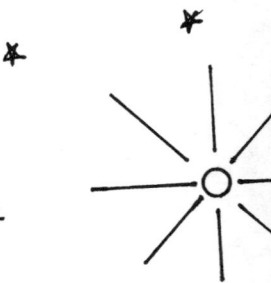

1. Basecoat gourd or potbelly with 1:1 mixture of Ice Blue and Liberty Blue. Basecoat feet with Burnt Orange and then Bronze. Lightly transfer on design.
2. Paint face, hair and beard. Right eye is based Green Sea. Float shading on left of iris with Deep River. Highlight with Thermal Green. Left eye is based Baby Blue and shaded with Avalon. Add Snow White twinkle stars to eyes. Cheeks are a Rouge wash.
3. Basecoat moon with Moon Yellow. Float shading on right side with Burnt Orange. Highlight left side with Scorching Yellow. Use the end of your paint brush dipped in Bronze for dots on the ends of the moon.
4. Basecoat the star with Blue Mist. Shade with Uniform Blue. Highlight with Snow White.
5. Area inside hood by hairline is Ice Blue. Add Burnt Orange and then go over with Bronze to the trim along hood and sleeves. Outline with Liberty Blue.
6. Float around hood with Baby Blue. Keep soft looking. Float Baby Blue highlights on forearms.
7. Basecoat mitts with Avalon. Shade with Liberty Blue and highlight with Baby Blue.
8. Float all shading on jacket with Ebony Black. Float under hood, around and inside arms, above feet, under beard and around star and moon.
9. Use a liner brush to make Snow White stars all over hood and jacket. Apply Snow White dots to centers of stars.
10. Brush over jacket with Frost Stars. Let dry well and spray varnish.

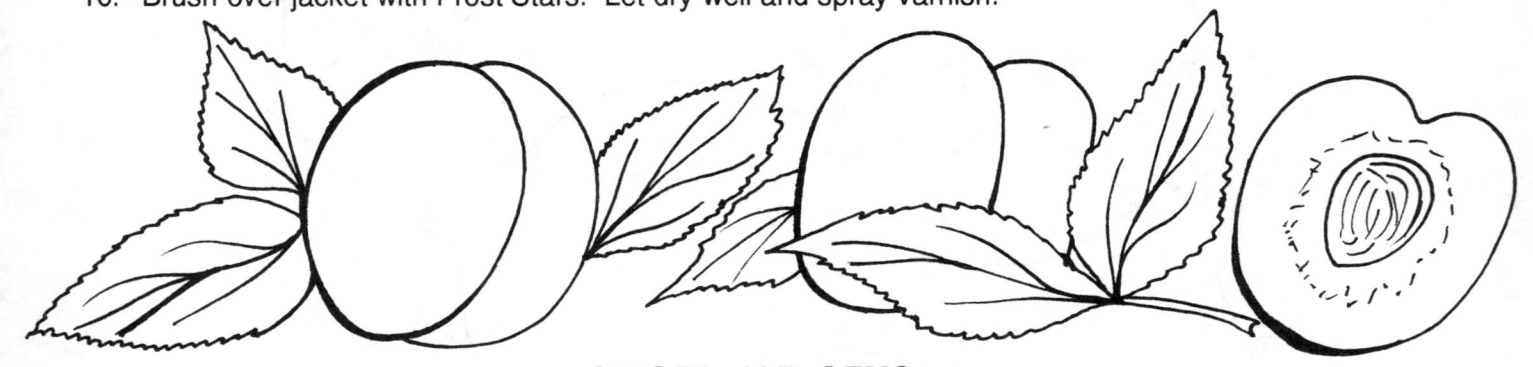

GINGER JAR GEMS

1. You will need a glass ginger jar lamp. Many stores now carry these lamps quite inexpensively, just for this purpose. Unscrew the bottom of the lamp and fill with collectibles of your choice. It's that easy!

2. I have chosen to fill mine with potpourri, wood shavings and scented wooden peaches.

3. These lamps look wonderful at Christmas filled to the brim with colorful festive candies. Use your imagination and have fun!

CANUCKY

PALETTE
Deco Art Americana
Country Red
Snow White
Calico Red
Deep Teal
Medium Flesh
Ebony Black
Leaf Green

Deco Art Hot Shots
Thermal Green

Delta Ceramcoat
Candy Bar
Quaker Grey
Green Sea
Rouge
Hippo Grey
Fleshtone
Deep River
Burnt Sienna

Accent Country Colors
Deep Forest Green
Raw Umber

1. Basecoat gourd Country Red. Basecoat feet Deep Forest Green. Lightly transfer on design.
2. Paint face, hair and beard. Eyes are based Green Sea, floated with Deep Forest Green. Cheeks are a Rouge wash.
3. Basecoat the flag Snow White. Then add Calico Red stripes and maple leaf. Outline leaf with Candy Bar. Float shading above fur area and base of leaf with Candy Bar as well. Shading on white flag area is floated Hippo Grey. Highlight Calico Red areas with Fiery Red. Use a liner brush to outline the flag with whip stitches using Ebony Black.
4. Markings on the feet are Snow White.
5. Basecoat mitts with Leaf Green. Float shading with Deep Forest Green. Highlight with Thermal Green.
6. Basecoat trees from left to right; Deep River, Leaf Green and Deep Teal. Use a dry deerfoot stippler to pounce on Snow White. Outline whip stitch with Ebony Black.
7. Use a rake brush to basecoat all fur areas on coat and hat with Hippo Grey.
8. Float shading around arms, all fur areas, flag and tree appliques and under beard and hairline with Candy Bar. This may take two coats. Use clean water so there is no halo effect and use a mop brush to soften lines.
9. Use a dry deerfoot stippler to pounce Quaker Grey over all fur areas. When dry go over with Snow White. Make sure to keep all three values showing.

DRIED APPLE WREATH

1. Slice unpeeled apples thinly. If you like them to stay white looking, dip them in an ascorbic acid solution. Ever-Fresh works well. I did not dip my apples on this particular wreath.

2. Lay apple slices out on trays and dry in dehydrator.

3. Spray varnish to discourage bugs.

4. Glue to a grapevine wreath on the right hand side. Glue a sprig of eucalyptus to the other side.

5. Spray the eucalyptus with a gold glitter spray.

CANUCKY

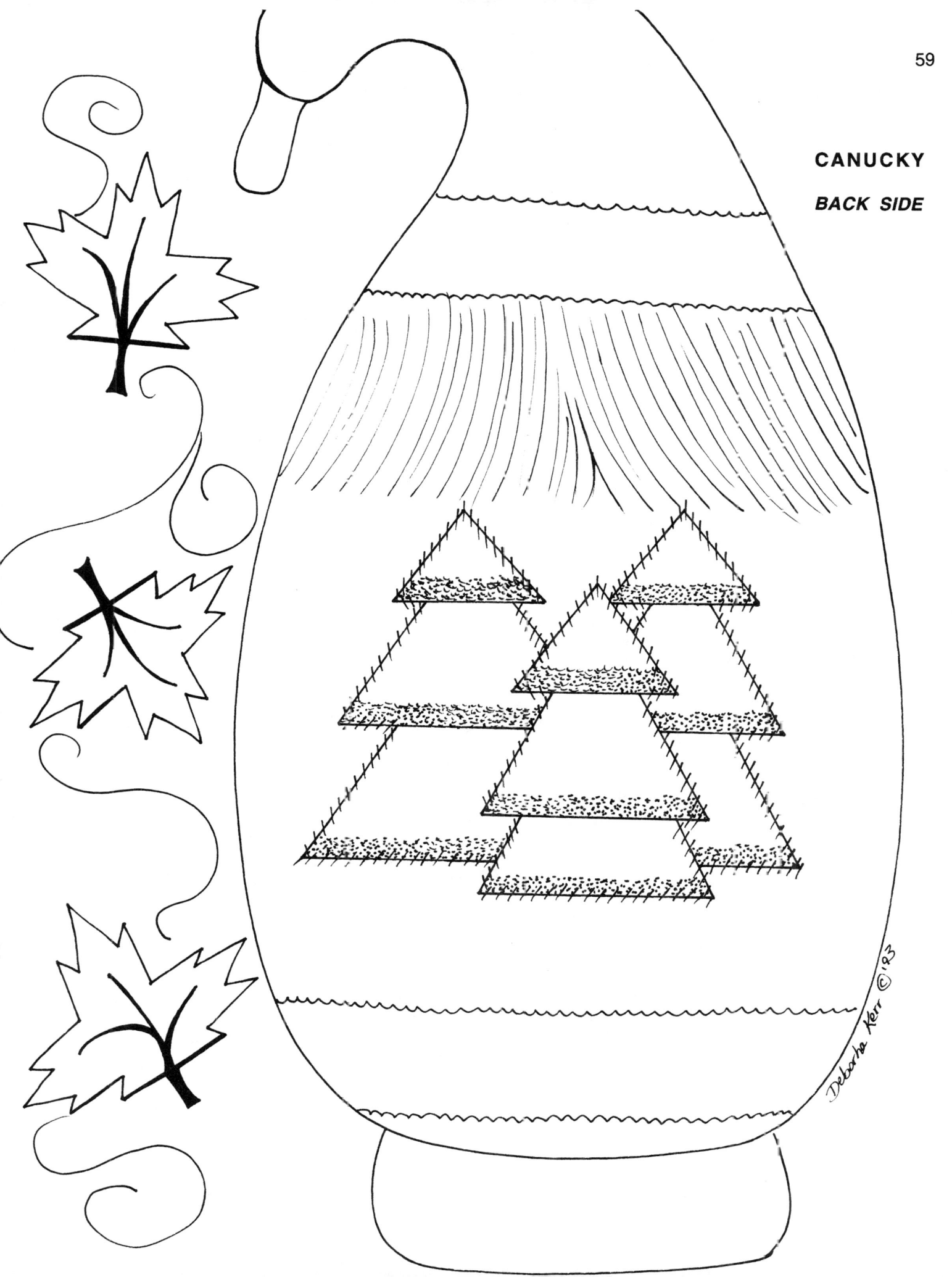

CANUCKY
BACK SIDE

UNCLE SAM

PALETTE
Deco Art Americana
Country Red Uniform Blue
Williamsburg Blue Ebony Black
Snow White Medium Flesh
Deco Art Dazzling Metallics
Venetian Gold
Accent Country Colors
Liberty Blue

1. Basecoat gourd Country Red. Draw a chalk line to indicate hat. Basecoat hat and feet Uniform Blue. Lightly transfer on design.
2. Paint face, hair and beard. Float under lower lip with Dark Flesh. Eyes are Williamsburg Blue floated with Liberty Blue. Cheeks are Country Red and Snow White wash.
3. Basecoat mitts Snow White. Shade with floated Uniform Blue.
4. Basecoat flag Country Red. Add Snow White stripes and square corner in Uniform Blue. Flag pole is Raw Umber. Knob is Venetian Gold. Outline flag with Raw Umber.
5. Float shading on hat above trim with Liberty Blue. Add Snow White stripe to trim.
6. Float shading on sleeves and feet with Liberty Blue. Highlight forearm area with Uniform Blue + a tad of Snow White.
7. Cut compressed sponge to indicated size. Dip in water and squeeze. Load in Snow White taking care to remove excess. Sponge stars on hat and sleeves.
8. Float shading on all Country Red areas such as bottom of hat trim, around arms, under beard, above shoes and to show leg definition on front and back.
9. Float Hippo Grey around flag and under trim area.
10. Use the other end of a paint brush dipped in Liberty Blue to make dotted trim around vest.
11. Spray varnish to finish.

I designed this handsome fellow as a tribute to my many wonderful American friends!

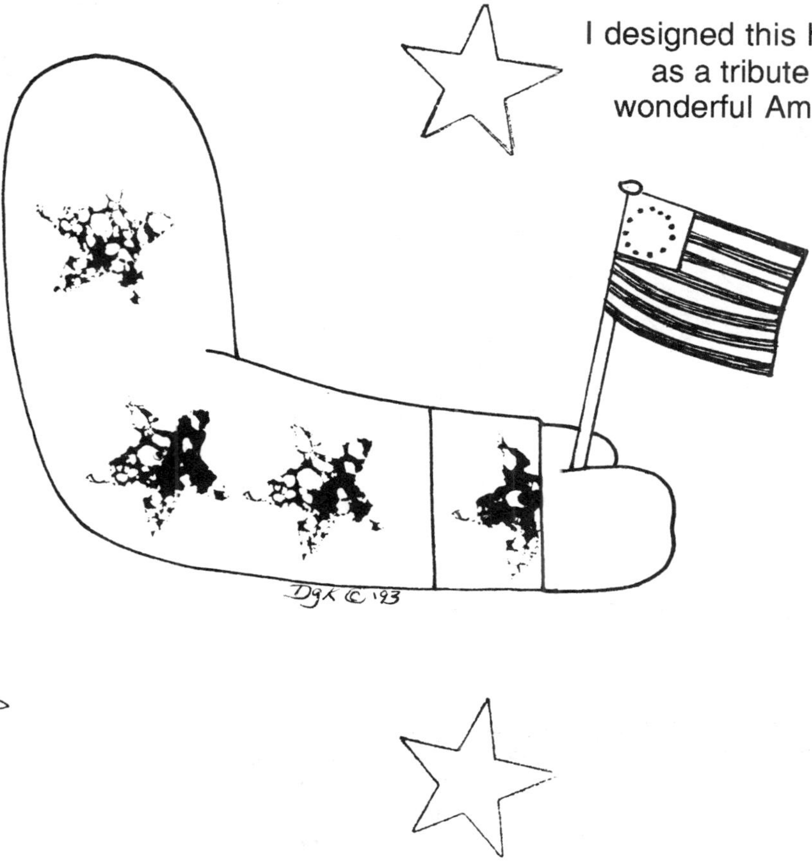

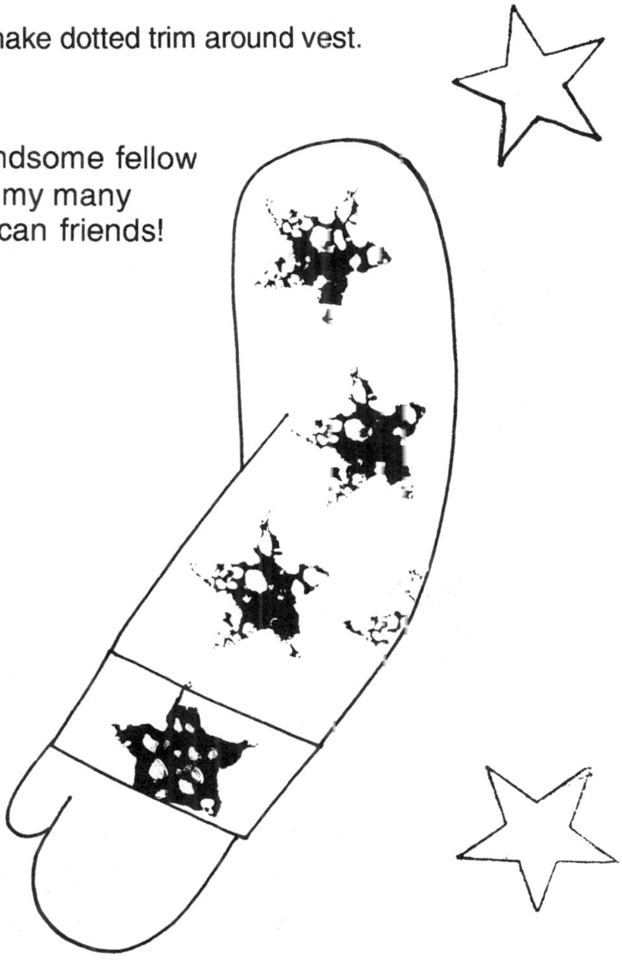

62

RED QUARTER

COUNTRY SAMPLER BASKET

BLUE QUARTER

63

GREEN QUARTER

YELLOW QUARTER

COUNTRY SAMPLER BASKET

PALETTE
Deco Art Americana
Country Blue Antique Gold Yellow Ochre
Country Red Soft Black Snow White
Slate Grey Raw Sienna Ultra Blue Deep
'Burnt Orange Burnt Umber
Deco Art Hot Shots
Torrid Orange Scorching Yellow
Fiery Red Thermal Green
Delta Ceramcoat
Candy Bar Charcoal
Green Sea Antique White
Accent Country Colors
Deep Forest Green
Folk Art
Lemonade

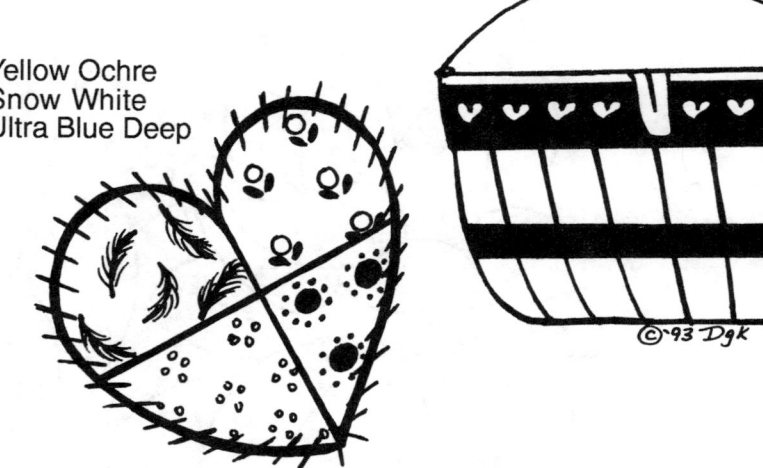

1. Sand basket. Seal entire basket except the inside with White Lightning. Seal underside of lid flaps as well.
2. Basecoat both strips around the outside of basket with Soft Black.
3. Quarter the basket by marking on a strip the same width as the middle wooden strip width. Basecoat both of the strips with Soft Black. When dry, sand strips lightly to allow some of the under color to come through. Basecoat the handle with Soft Black.
4. Basecoat each quarter respectively; County Red, Green Sea, Country Blue and Yellow Ochre. Lightly transfer on designs.
5. Basecoat one underside flap with Country Blue and the other with Green Sea.
6. Paint the scallop trim around the edge of the basket with Charcoal. Add decorative strokes with Deep Forest Green.
7. **Red Quarter**
   Basecoat rooster weathervane with Slate Grey. Float shading with Charcoal. Float highlights with Snow White. Float shading around outside of rooster with Candy Bar. Feathers on the background are liner strokes of Antique Gold.
8. **Green Quarter**
   Basecoat sunflowers with Yellow Ochre. Float shading to divide and create petals with Antique Gold. Outline with Burnt Umber. Highlight petals with Lemonade. Use a deerfoot stippler to pounce in centers with Burnt Umber. Float around this with Burnt Orange. Glaze over Burnt Orange with Torrid Orange thinned with water. Add dots to centers with Snow White and Scorching Yellow. Glaze sunflowers with Scorching Yellow wash and less Torrid Orange wash. Float around sunflowers with Deep Forest Green. Background is Deep Forest Green strokes and Country Red dots to form simple flowers.
9. **Blue Quarter**
   Basecoat pie plate with Snow White. Basecoat pie crust with Yellow Ochre. Float shading on crust with Raw Sienna. Add Burnt Umber here and there to strengthen. Use your liner brush to outline crust edging, holes and outside of crust with Burnt Umber. Glaze crust here and there with an Antique Gold wash. Drybrush highlights with Antique White. Float steam lines with Antique White. Keep them hazy looking. Float above and below pie plate edge with Country Blue. Float bottom of pie plate with County Blue as well. Strengthen with Ultra Blue Deep. Stipple Country Blue all over pie plate. Float Snow White on top of plate edge. Cut heart from compressed foam. Dip in water and squeeze out excess. Dip sponge in Ultra Blue Deep. Remove excess paint on paper towel. Add row of hearts to the pie plate. Float around pie with Ultra Blue Deep.
   Background is Snow White dots in a diamond pattern. Use the wooden end of your liner brush.
10. **Yellow Quarter**
    Basecoat tree trunk with Raw Sienna. Float shading with Burnt Umber. Highlight with Antique Gold. To create tree leaves first stipple with Deep Forest Green, then Green Sea, the Thermal Green, then less Antique Gold. Basecoat hearts with Country Red. Float left side of each heart with Fiery Red. Float right side with Candy Bar. Highlight with dry brush strokes of Snow White. Float behind right side of hearts with Deep Forest Green. Float around outside of tree with Antique Gold.
    Background is medium size dots of Country Blue outlined with a circle of smaller Snow White dots.
11. **TO FINISH**
    Paint hearts up the center of each Soft Black strip and around the outer edge of the sides of the basket. To make the hearts use the end of one of your larger brushes. Make two large dots, then draw down the tail with your stylus. Theses are often referred to as Dolly Parton hearts. Paint a large heart surrounded with small dots on the handle nob.

12. Spatter basket with thinned Soft Black. Spray varnish lightly. When dry brush the lid with Blending and Glazing Medium. Gently buff in Burnt Umber oil paint around the outside edge. Blend in with a mop brush until soft looking. Remove excess if necessary with thinner. Let dry overnight. Spray varnish. Remember to spray the underside of the basket flaps.

Paint dots around the top outside edge of the basket using Snow White. Spray with final coats of varnish.

TO LINE A BASKET

Cut a large circle out of your desired fabric. Stitch a baste line around the outer edge halfway around the circle. Cut threads and begin again around the remaining half. Gather each half into loose gathers. Place inside basket right side up. Use a white craft glue or Grumbacher Hyplar Matte Medium and Varnish. Workig a small area at a time turn stitch line of circle under. Spread glue on fabric and on basket. Slowly work your way around arranging gathers as you go. Secure with push pins until glue is set. Take your time, the results will be well worth it.

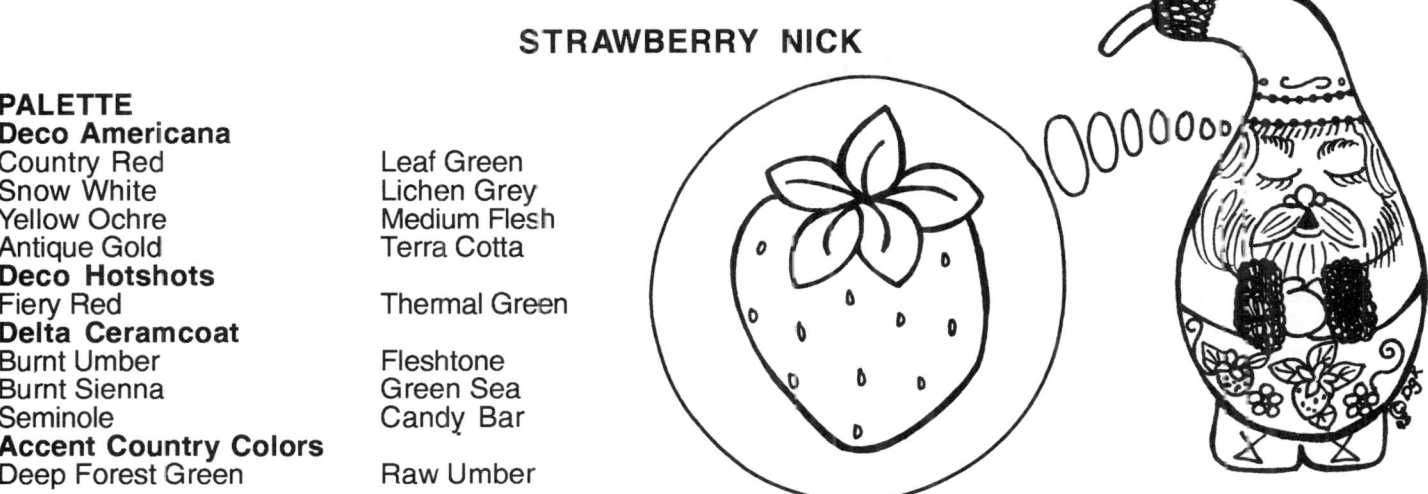

STRAWBERRY NICK

PALETTE
Deco Americana
Country Red   Leaf Green
Snow White   Lichen Grey
Yellow Ochre   Medium Flesh
Antique Gold   Terra Cotta
Deco Hotshots
Fiery Red   Thermal Green
Delta Ceramcoat
Burnt Umber   Fleshtone
Burnt Sienna   Green Sea
Seminole   Candy Bar
Accent Country Colors
Deep Forest Green   Raw Umber

1. Basecoat gourd or potbelly with Leaf Green. Feet are basecoated with Terra Cotta.
2. Lightly transfer on design. Paint face, hair and beard. Hair and bear are Burnt Umber, then Lichen Grey then Snow White. Eyes are Terra Cotta, floated with Burnt Umber. Cheeks and lips are thinned Country Red wash.
3. Basecoat strawberries with Country Red. Float tops with Candy Bar. Float undersides with Thermal Green. Add dry brush highlights with Fiery Red. Seeds are small specks of Antique Gold.
4. Basecoat strawberry bracts with Seminole. Float with Deep Forest Green. The leaves are basecoated with Green Sea. Float shading with Deep Forest Green. Add Deep Forest Green liner strokes for leaf divisions. Highlight with Thermal Green her and there.
6. Basecoat mittens with Antique Gold. Float shading with Terra Cotta. Highlight with Yellow Ochre.
7. Apply fur on jacket and hat by using a rake brush and Burnt Umber. When dry, pounce over using a deerfoot stippler dipped in Lichen Grey. Leave lots of Burnt Umber showing through.8. Basecoat hat band with Antique Gold. Float Terra Cotta along top of hat band. Add a row of Burnt Umber dots to top and bottom of hat band using the wooden end of your liner brush.
9. Float Deep Forest around and inside arms (except for upper forearm). Also float shading underneath beard and hairline, around mittens, hat band and fur. Use a mop brush to keep this soft looking. Highlight forearms with Thermal Green.
10. Apply scroll work to jacket and hat with Antique Gold. Add flowers using the wooden end of your brush. Each flower is five Snow White dots with a Country Red dot in the center.
11. Apply Raw Umber liner detail to the feet.
12. Finish with several coats of spray varnish.

STRAWBERRY NICK

STRAWBERRY NICK

BLOSSOMS

Deborha Kerr © '93

BLOSSOMS

PALETTE
Deco Art Americana
Raspberry
Snow White
Dark Chocolate
Medium Flesh
Ebony Black
Deep Teal
Delta Ceramacoat
Fleshtone
Burnt Sienna
Stonewedge
Hydrangea
Quaker Grey
Vintage Wine
Candy Bar
Light Ivory
Straw
Hippo Grey
Mendocino
Gamal Green
Accent Country Colors
Raw Umber
Folk Art
Heather

1. Basecoat gourd or potbelly Raspberry. Feet are Light Ivory.
2. Paint face, hair and beard. Eyes are Heather, floated with Vintage Wine. Cheeks are a wash mixture of Hydrangea + Raspberry 1:1.
3. Basecoat daisy Light Ivory. Float shading with Stonewedge. Tint petals with washes of Straw and Hydrangea. The daisy center is based Straw. Float around perimeter of center with Burnt Sienna. Add flecks of Dark Chocolate and Burnt Sienna. Stipple over all with Snow White. Leaves are Stonewedge Green. Float shading and outline with Gamal Green. Highlight with Deep Teal. Float around daisy on beard with Hippo Grey.
4. Basecoat mitts with Hydrangea. Float shading with Mendocino and highlight with Hydrangea + Snow White.
5. Trim on sleeves and hat are basecoated with Light Ivory. Add stylus dots with Hydrangea and Heather. Stitch marks are Mendocino.
6. Bows on feet are Mendocino. Stylus dots in centers are Hydrangea.
7. Float all shading on Raspberry areas such as above hat trim, inside sleeves, above feet, pockets, under beard and hair with Mendocino. This may take two layers. Keep soft looking. Use mop brush to blend.
8. Spray varnish to finish.

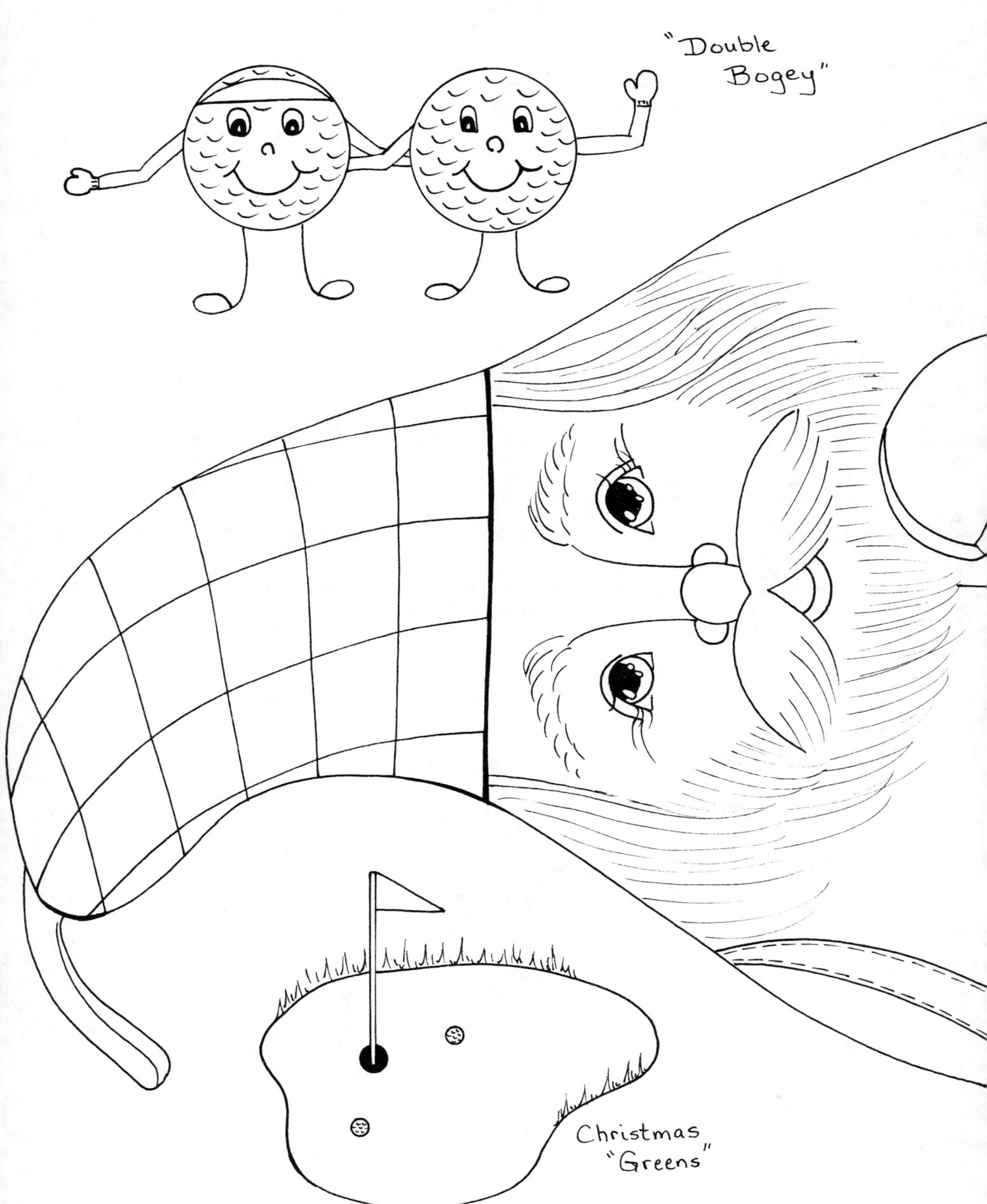

SAINT "NICKOLAS"

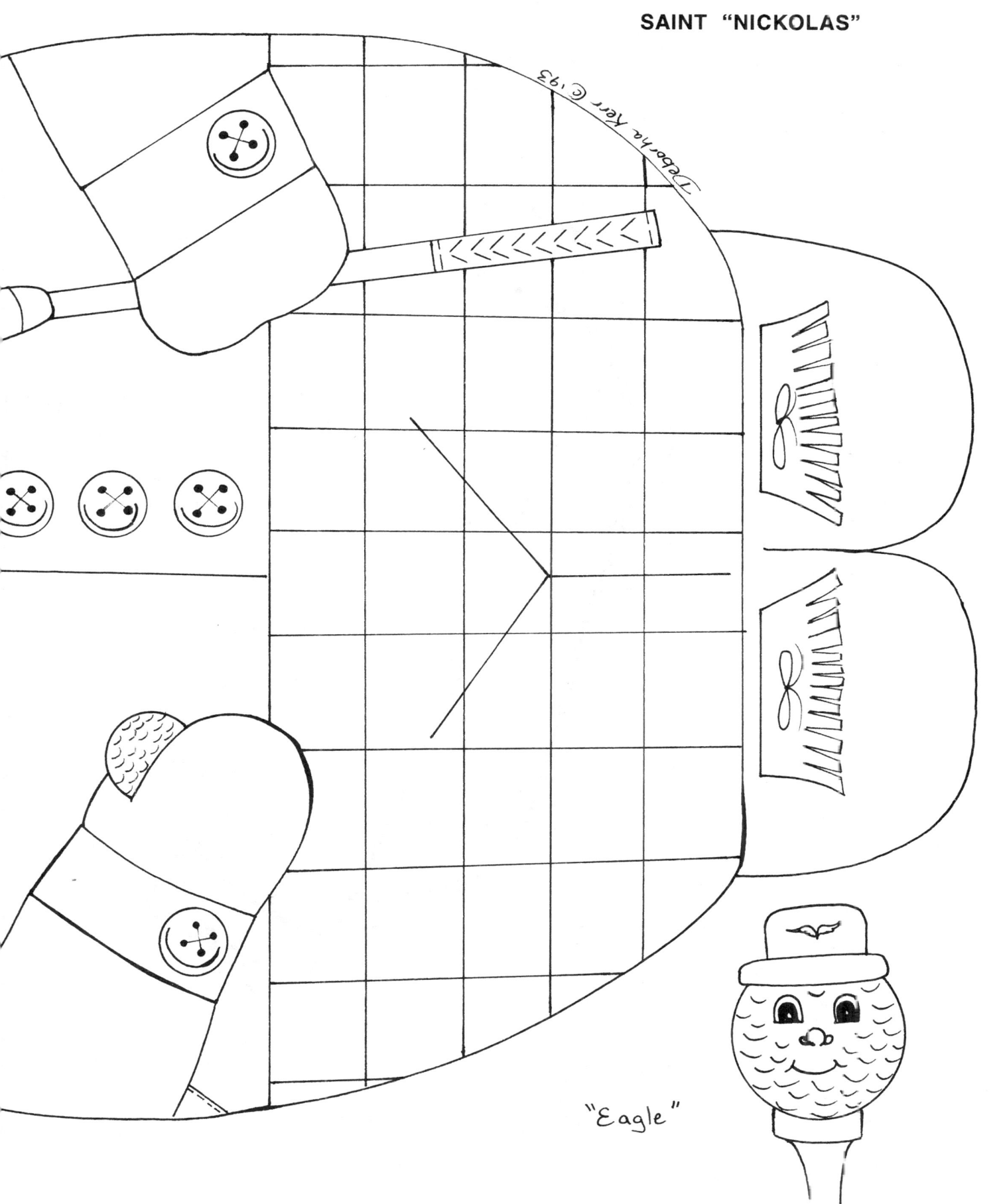

"Eagle"

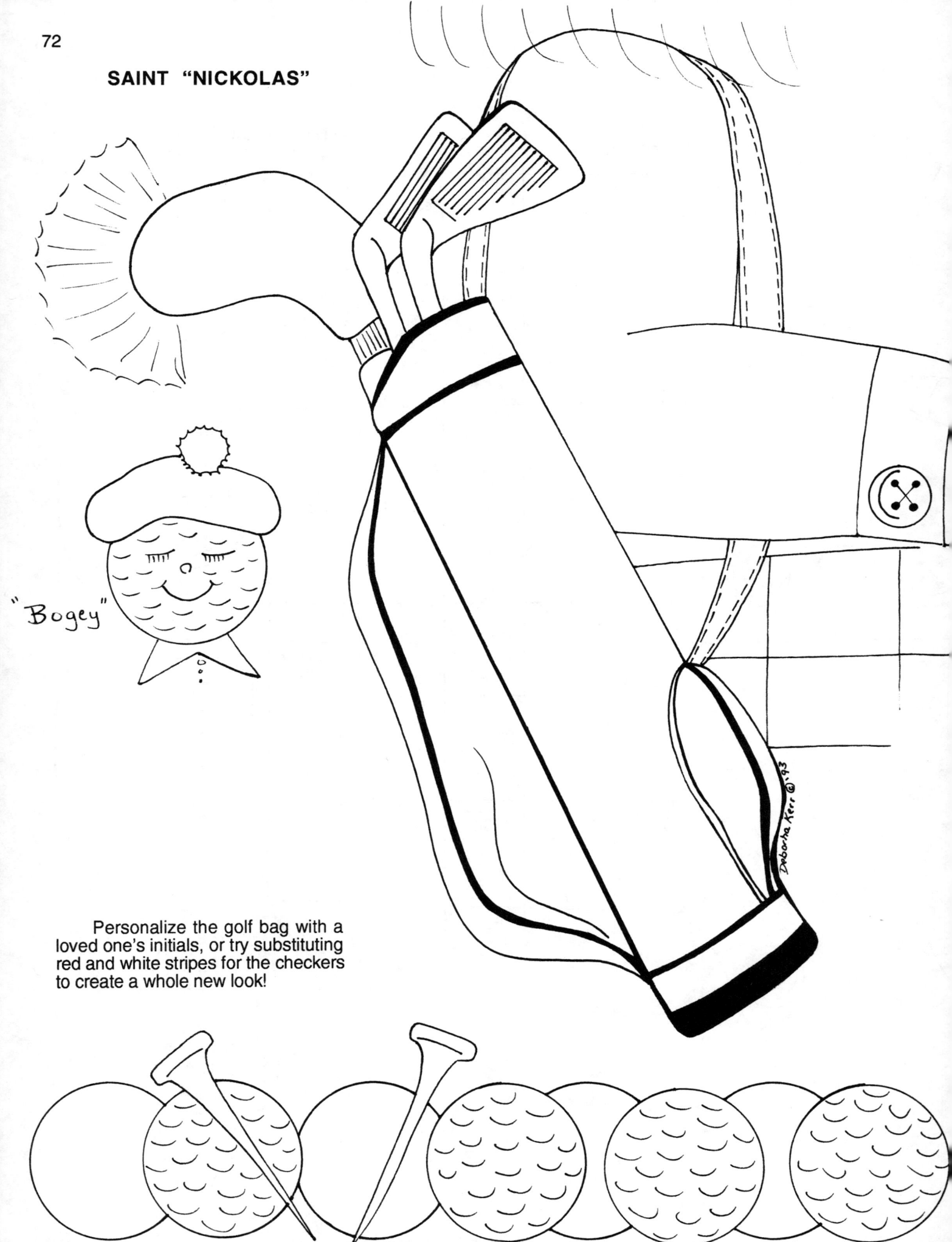

Everybody knows an enthusiastic golfer. Make this that extra special gift on your list!

"Birdie"

SAINT "NICKOLAS"

PALETTE
Deco Art Americana
Ebony Black
Leaf Green
Country Red
Moon Yellow
Taffy Cream
Snow White
Medium Flesh
Antique Gold
Terra Cotta

Deco Art Hot Shots
Scorching Yellow
Fiery Red
Thermal Green

Deco Art Dazzling Metallics
Shimmering Silver

Delta Ceramcoat
Candy Bar
Burnt Sienna
Hippo Grey
Black Green
Green Sea
Fleshtone
Quaker Grey

Accent Country Colors
Raw Umber
Deep Forest Green

1. Basecoat gourd Country Red. Basecoat feet with Ebony Black.
2. Use chalk to draw the bottom of the coat line while resting your hand on a counter and slowly turning the gourd. Bsecoat the coat with 2 or 3 coats of Moon Yellow. Lightly transfer on design.
3. Draw checkers on hat and pants freehand with chalk. Basecoat checkers alternately with Country Red and Leaf Green.
4. Paint face, hair and beard. Float Burnt Sienna shading under the hat line on the forehead. Eyes are basecoated Green Sea. Float with Deep Forest Green. Cheeks are a Country Red wash.
5. Float around the outline of the arms and inside the shoulder area with Terra Cotta. Highlight the upper forearm with Taffy Cream. Float the center line of the coat with Terra Cotta. Highlight the side by the buttons with Taffy Cream.
6. Basecoat the mittens with Snow White. Float shading with Hippo Grey. Basecoat the golf ball with Snow White. Float shading with Hippo Grey. Add Hippo Grey dimple marks.
7. Basecoat the golf bag with Terra Cotta. Float shading with Burnt Umber. Ribbing trim is also Burnt Umber. Use a fine liner to draw a faint line of Snow White down the center of ribbing. Float highlights on bag with Antique Gold down the center of the bag. Basecoat bag straps with Burnt Umber. Stitch lines are Snow White.
8. Basecoat the irons with Shimmering Silver. Float shading with Ebony Black. Line work details are also in Ebony Black.

    Basecoat club cover with Country Red. Stripe is Snow White. Stipple over cover using Snow White and your deerfoot stippler brush. Float shading with Candy Bar.

    Basecoat pompon with Snow White. Add Country Red liner strokes. Stipple over pompon lightly with Snow White.
9. Basecoat the wood club on the front with Terra Cotta. Float shading with Burnt Umber. Highlight with Antique Gold. Add Snow White liner work.
10. Outline every checker with Black Green. Float Black Green shading above the hat line and below the coat line. Float the leg definitions on the front and back of Santa. Float Black Green shading around the wood club shaft and around the golf bag where it overlaps the pants.
11. Basecoat the flaps on the shoes with Snow White. Add Ebony Black bows.
12. Basecoat buttons with Country Red. Float buttons with Candy Bar. Add Candy Bar dots. Highlight buttons with Fiery Red. Threadwork is Antique Gold.
13. Float shading on the bear behind the wood club with Hippo Grey.
14. Float Terra Cotta around everything that overlaps the coat. Lightly glaze the coat here and there with Scorching Yellow wash. Blend well so there are no lines. It will help to moisten the gourd first.
15. Brush highlights on every Leaf Green checker with Thermal Green.
16. Spray varnish with several coats to finish.

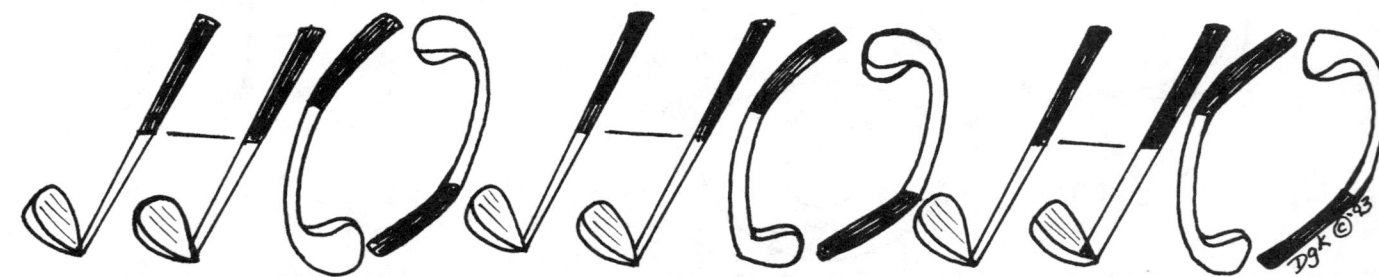

OIL BOOKS

	Vol.	Title	No.	Price
	Vol. 1	"His and Hers" by Susan Scheewe	101	$6.50 _____
	Vol. 5	"So Dear To My Heart" by Susan Scheewe	105	$5.50 _____
	Vol. 6	"Brushed With Elegance" by Susan Scheewe	106	$5.50 _____
	Vol. 7	"Paint 'n Patch" by Susan Scheewe	107	$5.50 _____
	Vol. 11	"I Love To Paint" by Susan Scheewe	111	$6.50 _____
	Vol. 14	"Enjoy Painting Animals" by Susan Scheewe	114	$6.50 _____
	Vol. 17	"Countryside Reflections" by Susan Scheewe	161	$6.50 _____
	Vol. 18	"Mostly Landscapes" by Susan Scheewe	216	$8.50 _____
	Vol. 19	"Gift of Painting" by Susan Scheewe...O/AC/WC	230	$8.50 _____
	Vol. 1	"Western Images" by Becky Anthony	186	$6.50 _____
	Vol. 3	"Fantasy Flowers II" by Georgia Bartlett	129	$6.50 _____
	Vol. 2	"Soft Petals" by Georgia Bartlett	171	$6.50 _____
	Vol. 6	"Painting Fantasy Flowers" by Georgia Bartlett	215	$7.50 _____
	Vol. 1	"Painting, A Barrel of Fun" by Donna Bell	194	$6.50 _____
	Vol. 2	"Painting, A Barrel of Fun" by Donna Bell	201	$7.50 _____
	Vol. 3	"Barnscapes and More" by Donna Bell	218	$8.50 _____
	Vol. 4	"Countryscapes" by Donna Bell	249	$8.50 _____
	Vol. 5	"Painter to Painter" by Donna Bell	263	$8.50 _____
NEW	Vol. 6	"Landscapes With Acrylics & Oil by Donna Bell	282	$8.50 _____
	Vol. 1	"Natures Palette" by Carol Binford ...O/AC	248	$8.50 _____
	Vol. 1	"Oil Painting The Easy Way" by Bill Blackman	219	$8.50 _____
	Vol. 1	"Mini Mini More" by Terri and Nancy Brown	150	$6.50 _____
	Vol. 2	"Mini Mini More" by Terri and Nancy Brown	151	$6.50 _____
	Vol. 4	"Heritage Trails" by Terri and Nancy Brown	169	$6.50 _____
NEW	Vol. 6	"Garden Trails" by Terri and Nancy Brown	283	$8.50 _____
	Vol. 1	"Windows of My World" by Jackie Clafin	174	$6.50 _____
	Vol. 2	"Windows of My World" by Jackie Clafin	181	$7.50 _____
	Vol. 3	"I'm Partial To Flowers" by Ellie Cook	157	$6.50 _____
	Vol. 2	"Expressions In Oil" by Delores Egger	154	$6.50 _____
	Vol. 4	"Expressions In Oil" by Delores Egger	239	$7.50 _____
	Vol. 1	"Victorian Days" by Gloria Gaffney	240	$8.50 _____
	Vol. 2	"Days of Heaven" by Gloria Gaffney	252	$8.50 _____
	Vol. 3	"Winter Song" by Gloria Gaffney	271	$8.50 _____
	Vol. 1	"Roses Are For Everyone" by Bill Huffaker	145	$7.50 _____
	Vol. 3	"Nature's Beauty" by Bill Huffaker	177	$6.50 _____
	Vol. 1	"Copper, Silver, Brass and Glass" by Susan Jenkins	211	$6.50 _____
	Vol. 1	"Backroads of My Memory" by Geri Kisner	225	$7.50 _____
	Vol. 2	"Backroads of My Memory" by Geri Kisner	245	$7.50 _____
	Vol. 1	"Country's Edge" by Shirley Koenig ...O/AC	179	$7.50 _____
	Vol. 2	"Country's Edge" by Shirley Koenig ...O/AC	212	$6.50 _____
	Vol. 1	"Ducks and Geese" by Jean Lyles	172	$6.50 _____
NEW	Vol. 1	"Pathway To Painting" by Lee McGowen	281	$8.50 _____
	Vol. 1	"Stepping Stones" by Judy Nutter	121	$6.50 _____
	Vol. 1	"Rustic Charms" by Sharon Rachal	175	$6.50 _____
	Vol. 2	"Rustic Charms II" by Sharon Rachal	199	$7.50 _____
	Vol. 3	"Rustic Charms III" by Sharon Rachal	217	$6.50 _____
	Vol. 4	"Rustic Charms IV" by Sharon Rachal	238	$7.50 _____
	Vol. 5	"Rustic Charms V, Florals" by Sharon Rachal	261	$8.50 _____
	Vol. 1	"Painting Flowers With Augie" by Augie Reis	152	$6.50 _____
	Vol. 1	"Realistic Florals and More" by Judy Sleight	233	$8.50 _____
	Vol. 2	"Painting Realism" by Judy Sleight	272	$8.50 _____
	Vol. 1	"Soft & Misty Paintings" by Kathy Snider	204	$8.50 _____
	Vol. 2	"Soft & Misty Paintings" by Kathy Snider	229	$8.50 _____
	Vol. 3	"Soft & Misty Paintings" by Kathy Snider	251	$8.50 _____
	Vol. 1	"More Old Friends" by Gene Waggoner	148	$6.50 _____
	Vol. 4	"Friends We've Known" by Gene Waggoner	187	$7.50 _____
	Vol. 5	"Friends Are Forever" by Gene Waggoner	231	$7.50 _____
	Vol. 1	"Fantasy Folk" by Don Weed	123	$6.50 _____
	Vol. 2	"Painting The Clowns by Don Weed	124	$6.50 _____
	Vol. 1	"Something Special For Everyone" by Mildred Yeiser	158	$6.50 _____
	Vol. 2	"Something Special For Everyone" by Mildred Yeiser	178	$6.50 _____
	Vol. 4	"Something Special For Everyone" by Mildred Yeiser	235	$7.50 _____
	Vol. 5	"Soft and Gentle Paintings" by Mildred Yeiser	268	$8.50 _____

FABRIC PAINTING BOOKS

Vol.	Title	No.	Price
Vol. 1	"Painting It's Our Bag" by Bev Hink/Susan Scheewe	193	$8.50 _____
Vol. 1	"Whimsical Critters" by Lori Ohlson	228	$7.50 _____
Vol. 1	"Oh Those Little Rascals" by Diane Permenter	247	$7.50 _____
Vol. 6	"Angels In My Stocking" by Diane Richards	254	$7.50 _____
Vol. 1	"Creations In Canvas and More" by Carol Spooner	256	$7.50 _____
Vol. 2	"Garden Gate" by Jolene Thompson	250	$7.50 _____
Vol. 5	"Count Your Blessings" by Chris Thornton	213	$8.50 _____
Vol. 6	"Share Your Blessings" by Chris Thornton	226	$8.50 _____
Vol. 5	"Daydreams and Sweet Shirts!!" by Don & Lynn Weed	208	$7.50 _____
Vol. 1	"Floral Fabrics and Watercolor" by Sally Williams	262	$8.50 _____

ACRYLIC BOOKS

	Vol.	Title	Page	Price
	Vol. 19	"Gift of Painting" by Susan Scheewe....O/AC/WC	230	$8.50 ___
	Vol. 1	"Painting It's Our Bag" by Bev Hink/Susan Scheewe	193	$8.50 ___
	Vol. 4	"Keepsake Sampler" by Susan & Camille Scheewe	200	$6.50 ___
	Vol. 1	"Loving You" by Susan & Camille Scheewe	244	$7.50 ___
NEW	Vol. 1	"Keepsakes For The Holidays" by Charleen Stempel & Susan Scheewe	286	$8.50 ___
	Vol. 1	"Kids and Water" by Joyce Benner	234	$8.50 ___
	Vol. 1	"Natures Palette" by Carol Binford	248	$8.50 ___
	Vol. 1	"Santas and Sams" by Bobi Dolara	258	$8.50 ___
	Vol. 2	"Vintage Peace" by Bobi Dolara	270	$8.50 ___
	Vol. 1	"Holiday Gathering" by Angie Hupp	267	$8.50 ___
	Vol. 1	"Happy Heart, Happy Home" by Cathy Jones	241	$7.50 ___
NEW	Vol. 1	"Festive Collectibles" by Deborha Kerr	279	$8.50 ___
	Vol. 1	"Country's Edge" by Shirley Koenig......O/AC	179	$7.50 ___
	Vol. 2	"Country's Edge" by Shirley Koenig......O/AC	212	$6.50 ___
	Vol. 1	"Huckleberry Horse" by Hanna Long	269	$8.50 ___
	Vol. 1	"Love Lives Here" by Mary Lynn Lewis	170	$6.50 ___
	Vol. 2	"Love Lives Here" by Mary Lynn Lewis	185	$6.50 ___
	Vol. 3	"Love Lives Here" by Mary Lynn Lewis	195	$6.50 ___
NEW	Vol. 1	"Special Welcomes" by Corinne Miller	287	$8.50 ___
NEW	Vol 1	"Fruit & Flower Fantasies" by Joyce Morrison	277	$8.50 ___
	Vol. 1	"Wildflower Sampler" by Bev Norman	191	$8.50 ___
	Vol. 1	"Whimsical Critters" by Lori Ohlson	228	$7.50 ___
	Vol. 1	"Holiday Medley" by Nina Owens	265	$8.50 ___
	Vol. 1	"Oh Those Little Rascals" by Diane Permenter	247	$7.50 ___
	Vol. 1	"Forever In My Heart" by Diane Richards.....AC/FABRIC	188	$6.50 ___
	Vol. 2	"Memories In My Heart" by Diane Richards..AC/FABRIC	189	$6.50 ___
	Vol. 3	"Forever In My Heart II" by Diane Richards...AC/FABRIC	205	$7.50 ___
	Vol. 5	"Memories In Your Heart" by Diane Richards	237	$7.50 ___
	Vol. 6	"Angels In My Stocking" by Diane Richards	254	$7.50 ___
	Vol. 7	"Nostalgic Dreams" by Diane Richards	273	$8.50 ___
	Vol. 1	"Creations in Canvas...and More" by Carol Spooner	256	$7.50 ___
NEW	Vol. 1	"Christmas Visions" by Max Terry	278	$8.50 ___
NEW	Vol. 2	"Christmas Presence" by Max Terry	285	$8.50 ___
	Vol. 1	"Country Primitives" by Maxine Thomas	274	$8.50 ___
	Vol. 1	"Rise and Shine" by Jolene Thompson	214	$6.50 ___
	Vol. 2	"Garden Gate" by Jolene Thompson	250	$7.50 ___
	Vol. 1	"Count Your Blessings" by Chris Thornton	176	$8.50 ___
	Vol. 3	"Count Your Blessings" by Chris Thornton	196	$6.50 ___
	Vol. 5	"Count Your Blessings" by Chris Thornton	213	$8.50 ___
	Vol. 6	"Share Your Blessings" by Chris Thornton	226	$8.50 ___
	Vol. 7	"Blessings" by Chris Thornton	255	$8.50 ___
	Vol. 8	"Christmas Blessings" by Chris Thornton	266	$8.50 ___
NEW	Vol. 9	"Blessings For The Home" by Chris Thornton	275	$8.50 ___
	Vol. 5	"Daydreams & Sweet Shirts II" by Don & Lynn Weed	208	$7.50 ___
	Vol. 1	"Floral Fabrics and Watercolor" by Sally Williams	262	$8.50 ___
	Vol. 1	"Friendship Garden" by Shirley Wingert	253	$8.50 ___

WATERCOLOR BOOKS

	Vol.	Title	Page	Price
	Vol. 20	"Simply Country Watercolors" by Susan Scheewe	257	$8.50 ___
	Vol. 21	"Simply Watercolor" by Susan Scheewe...TV Book	260	$11.95 ___
NEW	Vol. 22	"Watercolor For Everyone" by Susan Scheewe...T.V. Book	276	$11.95 ___
	Vol. 4	"Enjoy Watercolor" by Ellie Cook	210	$7.50 ___
	Vol. 6	"Watercolor Memories" by Ellie Cook	246	$7.50 ___
	Vol. 1	"The Way I Started" by Gary Hawk	120	$6.00 ___
	Vol. 2	"Anyone Can Watercolor" by Ken Johnston	118	$6.50 ___
	Vol. 1	"Watercolor Fun and Easy" by Beverly Kaiser	243	$7.50 ___
NEW	Vol. 1	"Flowers, Ribbon and Lace in Watercolor" by Lynda McCulloch	280	$8.50 ___
	Vol. 1	"Floral Fabrics and Watercolor" by Sally Williams	262	$8.50 ___

PEN AND INK BOOKS / COLORED PENCIL BOOKS

	Vol.	Title	Page	Price
	Vol. 2	"Barnyards and Billygoats" by Claudia Nice	134	$6.50 ___
	Vol. 3	"Wing and Wildflowers" by Claudia Nice	135	$6.50 ___
	Vol. 6	"Journey of Memories" by Claudia Nice	166	$6.50 ___
	Vol. 7	"Scenes from Seasons Past" by Claudia Nice	183	$8.50 ___
	Vol. 8	"Taste of Summer" by Claudia Nice	223	$8.50 ___
NEW	Vol. 9	"Familiar Faces" by Claudia Nice	284	$8.50 ___
	Vol. 1	"Colored Pencil Made Easy" by Jane Wunder	232	$7.50 ___
	Vol. 2	"Colored Pencil Made Easy" by Jane Wunder	242	$7.50 ___
	Vol. 3	"The Beauty of Colored Pencil and Ink Drawing" by Jane Wunder	259	$7.50 ___

VIDEOS

"The Gift Of Painting, Simply Watercolor"
By Susan Scheewe Brown. Guided instruction through tools and techniques for the beginning watercolorist...............$24.95

"The Gift Of Painting"
By Susan Scheewe Brown. Problems and solutions when painting oil landscapes. The video runs 90-minutes while two landscapes are completed........................$24.95

"Painting For The Holidays"
By Susan Scheewe Brown Have fun with Sue during this 60 minute as she shares ideas and inspiration for holiday greeting cards. $24.95

****
SHIPPING & HANDLING CHARGES

Add $2.00 for the First Book for shipping and handling.

Add $1.50 per each additional book.

Please Add $3.00 for handling & postage, PER TAPE. Sorry we must have a "NO REFUND-NO RETURN " policy.

U.S. CURRENCY

PRICES SUBJECT TO CHANGE WITHOUT NOTICE

Rev. 11-9-93

SUSAN SCHEEWE PUBLICATIONS
13435 N.E. WHITAKER WAY PORTLAND, OR. 97230
PH. (503) 254-9100 FAX (503) 252-9508

GHOST SHELLS
Pages 36, 45

FROSTED FOREST
Pages 32,33

FROSTY BLUES
Pages 29,30,32